Venture Deals

Venture Deals

BE SMARTER THAN YOUR LAWYER AND VENTURE CAPITALIST

Second Edition

Brad Feld
Jason Mendelson

WILEY

John Wiley & Sons, Inc.

Published by John Wiley & Sons, Inc., Hoboken, New Jersey.
Published simultaneously in Canada.

For general information on our other products and services or for technical support, please contact our Customer Care Department within the United States at (800) 762-2974, outside the United States at (317) 572-3993 or fax (317) 572-4002.

Wiley publishes in a variety of print and electronic formats and by print-on-demand. Some material included with standard print versions of this book may not be included in e-books or in print-on-demand. If this book refers to media such as a CD or DVD that is not included in the version you purchased, you may download this material at http://booksupport.wiley.com. For more information about Wiley products, visit www.wiley.com.

978-1-118-44361-3

Printed in the United States of America

10

To the best fathers on the planet:
Robert Mendelson and Stanley Feld.

Contents

Foreword

I wish I'd had this book when I started my first company. At the time, I didn't know preferred stock from chicken stock and thought a right of first refusal was something that applied to the NFL waiver wire.

Today, as the CEO of Twitter and the founder of three previous companies, the latter two acquired by public companies and the first acquired by a private company, I've learned many of the concepts and lessons in this book the hard way. While I had some great investors and advisers along the way, I still had to figure out all the tricks, traps, and nuances on my own.

My partners and I in our first company, Burning Door Networked Media, were novices so we made a lot of mistakes, but we managed to sell the company in 1996 for enough money to keep ourselves knee-deep in Starbucks tall coffees every morning for a year.

Several years later, my partners at Burning Door and I started a new company called Spyonit. This company did better and was sold to a public company called 724 Solutions in September 2000. Our stock was tied up for a year (we weren't that tuned into registration rights at the time) and when we got our hands on the stock in mid-September 2001, the collapse of the Internet bubble and the financial aftermath of 9/11 had caused our stock to decline to the point that it was worth enough money to keep us knee-deep in tall skim lattes at Starbucks every morning for a year.

So, like all good entrepreneurs, we tried again. This time, armed with a lot more knowledge and humility, we started FeedBurner in 2004. We raised several rounds of venture capital, including a seed round from DFJ Portage, a Series A round from Mobius Venture Capital (the firm Brad Feld and Jason Mendelson were part of at the time) and Sutter Hill, and a Series B round from Union Square Ventures. FeedBurner grew quickly, and before we knew it we had attracted acquisition interest from several companies, including

Google, which purchased us in 2007 and allowed me to stop using coffee-purchase analogies to quantify the payout.

After spending several years at Google, I was recruited to join Twitter, where I now am the CEO. During my tenure with the company, Twitter has grown dramatically, from 50 people to more than 430 people, and has completed two major rounds of financing, having raised over $250 million.

When I reflect back on what I now know about VC deals, acquisitions, how VCs work, and how to negotiate, it's very satisfying to see how far I've come from that day back in the early 1990s when I co-founded Burning Door Networked Media. When I read through this book, I kept thinking over and over, "Where were you when I started out?" as the knowledge contained between these covers would have saved me a remarkable amount of time and money on my journey.

Brad and Jason have written a book that is hugely important for any aspiring entrepreneurs, students, and first-time entrepreneurs. But it's not just limited to them—as I read through it I found new pearls of wisdom that even with all the experience I have today I can put to good use. And if you are a VC or aspire to be a VC, get in the front of the line to read this to make sure you are armed with a full range of understanding of the dynamics of your business. Finally, if you are a lawyer who does these deals for a living, do yourself a favor and read this also, if only to be armed with things to use to torture your adversaries.

Dick Costolo
Twitter CEO
March 2011

Preface

One of the ways to finance a company is to raise venture capital. While only a small percentage of companies raise venture capital, many of the great technology companies that have been created, including Google, Apple, Cisco Systems, Yahoo!, Netscape, Sun Microsystems, Compaq, Digital Equipment Corporation, and America Online (AOL) raised venture capital early in their lives. Some of today's fastest-growing entrepreneurial companies, such as Facebook, Twitter, LinkedIn, Zynga, and Groupon, were also recipients of venture capital.

Over the past 17 years we've been involved in hundreds of venture capital financings. Seven years ago, after a particularly challenging financing, we decided to write a series of blog posts that would demystify the venture capital financing process. The result was the Term Sheet Series on Brad's blog (www.feld.com/wp/category/termsheet), which was the inspiration for this book.

As each new generation of entrepreneurs emerges, there is a renewed interest in how venture capital deals come together. We encounter many of these first-time entrepreneurs through our activities as venture capitalists at our firm Foundry Group (www.foundrygroup.com), as well as our involvement in TechStars (www.techstars.com). We have been regularly reminded that there is no definitive guide to venture capital deals and as a result set out to create one.

In addition to describing venture capital deals in depth, we've tried to create context around the players, the deal dynamics, and how venture capital funds work. We've tossed in a section on negotiation, if only to provide another viewpoint into the brains of how a venture capitalist (at least the two of us) might think about negotiation. We also took on explaining the other term sheet that fortunate entrepreneurs will encounter—namely the letter of intent to acquire your company.

We've tried to take a balanced view between the entrepreneurs' perspective and the venture capitalists' perspective. As early stage investors, we know we are biased toward an early stage perspective, but we try to provide context that will apply to any financing stage. We've also tried to make fun of lawyers any chance we get.

We hope you find this book useful in your quest to create a great company.

Audience

When we first conceived this book, we planned to target it at first-time entrepreneurs. We both have a long history of funding and working with first-time entrepreneurs and often learn more from them than they learn from us. Through our involvement in TechStars, we've heard a wide range of questions about financings and venture capital from first-time entrepreneurs. We've tried to do a comprehensive job of addressing those questions in this book.

As we wrote the book, we realized it was also useful for experienced entrepreneurs. A number of the entrepreneurs who read early drafts or heard about what we were writing gave us feedback that they wished a book like this had existed when they were starting their first company. When we asked the question "Would this be useful for you today?" many said, "Yes, absolutely." Several sections, including the ones on negotiation and how venture capital funds work, were inspired by long dinner conversations with experienced entrepreneurs who told us that we had to write this stuff down, either on our blog or in a book. Well—here it is!

Of course, before one becomes a first-time entrepreneur, one is often an aspiring entrepreneur. This book is equally relevant for the aspiring entrepreneur of whatever age. In addition, anyone in school who is interested in entrepreneurship—whether in business school, law school, an undergraduate program, or an advanced degree program—should benefit from this book. We've both taught many classes on various topics covered in this book and hope this becomes standard reading for any class on entrepreneurship.

We were once inexperienced venture capitalists. We learned mostly by paying attention to more experienced venture capitalists, as well as actively engaging in deals. We hope this book becomes another tool in the tool chest for any young or aspiring venture capitalist.

While we've aimed the book at entrepreneurs, we hope that even lawyers (especially those who don't have much experience doing venture capital deals) and experienced venture capitalists will benefit from us putting these thoughts down in one place. At the minimum, we hope they recommend the book to their less experienced colleagues.

In an early draft, we varied gender on pronouns, using "she" liberally throughout the book. However, as we edited the book, we found that the mixed gender was confusing and made the book less readable. So we decided to use male pronouns throughout as a generic pronoun for both genders. We are sensitive to gender issues in both computer science and entrepreneurship in general—Brad has worked for a number of years as chair of the National Center for Women and Information Technology (www.ncwit.org). We hope our female readers are okay with this approach and hope someday someone comes up with a true gender-neutral set of English pronouns.

Finally, unintended beneficiaries of this book are the spouses of venture capitalists, lawyers, and entrepreneurs, especially those entrepreneurs actively involved in a deal. While Brad's wife Amy is quick to say, "Everything I've learned about venture capital has come from overhearing your phone calls," we hope other spouses can dip into this book every now and then. This can be especially useful when your spouse needs some empathy while complaining about how his venture capitalist is trying to jam a participating preferred down his throat.

Overview of the Contents

We start off with a brief history of the venture capital term sheet and a discussion of the different parties who participate in venture capital transactions.

We then discuss how to raise money from a venture capitalist, including determining how much money an entrepreneur should raise and what types of materials one will need before hitting the fundraising trail. Included in this section is a discussion about the process that many venture capitalists follow to decide which companies to fund.

We then dive deeply into the particular terms that are included in venture capital term sheets. We've separated this into three chapters—terms related to economics, terms related to control, and all of the other terms. We strive to give a balanced view of the particular terms along with strategies to getting to a fair deal.

Following the chapters on terms, we discuss how convertible works and then go into a frank discussion about how venture capital firms operate, including how venture capitalists are motivated and compensated. We then discuss how these structural realities can impact a company's chance of getting funded or could impact the relationship between the venture capitalist, his firm, and the entrepreneur after the investment is made.

Since the process of funding involves a lot of negotiation, the book contains a primer on negotiations and how particular strategies may work better or worse in the venture capital world. We also attempt to help the entrepreneur learn ways to consummate a transaction in a venture capital financing while avoiding common mistakes and pitfalls.

Since there is no such thing as a standard venture capital financing, we cover different issues to consider that depend on the stage of financing a company is raising.

As a bonus, we've tossed in a chapter about the other important term sheet that entrepreneurs need to know about: the letter of intent to acquire your company.

Finally, we end with tips concerning several common legal issues that most startups face. While not a dissertation on everything an entrepreneur needs to know, we've tried to include a few important things that we think entrepreneurs should pay attention to.

Throughout the book we've enlisted a close friend and longtime entrepreneur, Matt Blumberg, the CEO of Return Path, to add his perspective. Whenever you see a sidebar titled "The Entrepreneur's Perspective," these are comments from Matt on the previous section.

Additional Materials

Along with this book, we've created some additional materials that you may want to review. They are all on the AsktheVC web site at www.askthevc.com.

AsktheVC started out several years ago as a question-and-answer site that we managed. We've recently added a new section called "Resources" where the reader can find many standard forms of documents that are used in venture financings. They include the term sheet as well as all of the documents that are generated from the term sheet as part of a venture financing.

We have included the standard forms that we use at Foundry Group (yes, you can use these if we ever finance your company). We've also included links for the most popular standard documents that are used in the industry today, along with commentary about some of the advantages and disadvantages of using them.

Additional resources for classroom use are available to professors. Please visit www.wiley.com/WileyCDA/WileyTitle/productCd-1118443616.html for more information.

Jason Mendelson and Brad Feld
October 2012

Acknowledgments

We wouldn't have been able to write this book without the able assistance of many people.

A huge thanks goes to Matt Blumberg, CEO of Return Path, for all of his insightful and entrepreneur-focused comments. Matt provided all of the sidebars for "The Entrepreneur's Perspective" throughout the book, and his comments helped focus us (and hopefully you) on the key issues from an entrepreneur's perspective.

Our Foundry Group partners, Seth Levine and Ryan McIntyre, put up with us whenever Brad said, "I'm working on Jason's book again," and whenever Jason said, "I'm working on Brad's book again." Our assistants, Kelly Collins and Jill Spruiell, as always, were invaluable to us on this project, and we appreciate the support of the rest of the crew at the Foundry Group. You guys are the best team anyone could ever have.

A number of friends, colleagues, and mentors reviewed early drafts of the book and gave us extensive feedback. Thanks to the following for taking the time to meaningfully improve this book: Amy Batchelor, Raj Bhargava, Jeff Clavier, Greg Gottesman, Brian Grayson, Douglas Horch, David Jilk, TA McCann, George Mulhern, Wiley Nelson, Heidi Roizen, Ken Tucker, and Jud Valeski.

Jack Tankersley, one of the fathers of the Colorado venture capital industry, provided a number of his early deal books from his time at Centennial Funds. In addition to being fascinating history on some legendary early venture capital deals, they confirmed that the term sheet hasn't evolved much over the past 30 years. We'd also like to thank Jack for the extensive comments he made on an early draft of the book.

Thanks to Bill Aulet and Patricia Fuligni of the MIT Entrepreneurship Center for helping track down the original Digital Equipment Corporation correspondence between Ken Olson and Georges Doriot.

Our VC brethren, whether they realize it or not, have had a huge impact on this book. The ones we've learned from—both good and bad—are too numerous to list. But we want to thank them all for participating with us on our journey to help create amazing companies. We can't think of anything we'd rather be doing professionally, and we learn something new from you every day.

We've worked with many lawyers over the years, many of whom have taken us to school on various topics in this book. We thank you for all of your help, advice, education, and entertainment. We'd especially like to thank our friends Eric Jensen and Mike Platt at Cooley LLP, who have consistently helped us during the fog of a negotiation. Eric was Jason's mentor, boss, and friend while at Cooley and originally taught Jason how all of this worked.

We'd like to thank one of Brad's original mentors, Len Fassler, for creating the spark that initiated this book. Len's introduction to Matthew Kissner, a board member at John Wiley & Sons, resulted in a two-book contract with Wiley, which included *Do More Faster: TechStars Lessons to Accelerate Your Startup* by Brad and David Cohen. Although *Do More Faster* was published first, the idea for this book was the one that originally captured the attention of several people at Wiley.

Brad would like to thank Pink Floyd for *The Dark Side of the Moon* and *Wish You Were Here*, two albums that kept him going throughout the seemingly endless "read through and edit this just one more time" cycle. He'd also like to thank the great staff at Canyon Ranch in Tucson for giving him a quiet place to work for the last week before the "final final draft" was due.

Jason would like to thank the University of Colorado Law School and especially Brad Bernthal and Phil Weiser for letting him subject himself to both law and business students while teaching many of the subjects contained in this book. Special thanks to Herbie Hancock for providing the background music while Jason worked on this book.

A number of friends and colleagues found errors in the first edition, which we dutifully listed at www.askthevc.com/wp/errata. Special thanks go to David Cohen, Anurag Mehta, Tom Godin, Philip Lee, Tal Adler, and Jason Seats, who were the first to identify each error.

Finally, we thank all of the entrepreneurs we have ever had the chance to work with. Without you, we have nothing to do. Hopefully we have made you proud in our attempt to amalgamate in this book all of the collective wisdom we gained from working with you.

The Art of the Term Sheet

One of the first famous venture capital investments was Digital Equipment Corporation (DEC). In 1957 American Research and Development Corporation (AR&D), one of the first venture capital firms, invested $70,000 in DEC. When DEC went public in 1968, this investment was worth over $355 million, or a return of over 5,000 times the invested capital. AR&D's investment in DEC was one of the original venture capital home runs.

In 1957 the venture capital industry was just being created. At the time, the investor community in the United States was uninterested in investing in computer companies, as the last wave of computer-related startups had performed poorly and even large companies were having difficulty making money in the computer business. We can envision the frustration of DEC's co-founders, Ken Olson and Harlan Anderson, as the investors they talked to rejected them and their fledgling idea for a business. We can also imagine their joy when Georges Doriot, the founder of American Research and Development Corporation, offered to fund them. After a number of conversations and meetings, Doriot sent Olson and Anderson a letter expressing his interest in investing, along with his proposed terms. Today, this document is called the *term sheet*.

Now, imagine what that term sheet looked like. There are three different possibilities. The first is that it was a typed one-page letter that said, "We would like to invest $70,000 in your company and buy 78 percent of it." The next is that it was two pages of legal terms that basically said, "We would like to invest $70,000 in your company and buy 78 percent of it." Or it could have been an eight-page typed document that had all kinds of *protective provisions*, vesting arrangements, *drag-along rights*, and Securities and Exchange Commission (SEC) registration rights.

Our guess is that it was not the third option. Over the past 50 years, the art of the term sheet has evolved and expanded, reaching its current eight- (or so) page literary masterpiece. These eight pages contain a lot more than "We'd like to invest $X in your company and get Y percent of it," but, as you'll learn, there really are only two key things that matter in the actual term sheet negotiation—*economics* and *control*.

In DEC's case, by owning 78 percent of the company, AR&D effectively had control of the company. And the price was clearly defined—$70,000 bought 78 percent of the company, resulting in a $90,000 *postmoney* valuation.

Today's venture capital investments have many more nuances. Individual *venture capitalists* (VCs) usually end up owning less than 50 percent of the company, so they don't have effective voting control but often negotiate provisions that give them control over major decisions by the company. Many companies end up with multiple venture capitalists who invest in the company at different points in time, resulting in different ownership percentages, varying rights, and diverging motivations. Founders don't always stay with the company through the exit and, in some cases, they end up leaving relatively early in the life of a company for a variety of reasons. Companies fail, and venture capitalists have gotten much more focused on protecting themselves for the downside as well as participating in the upside. Governance issues are always complex, especially when you have a lot of people sitting around the negotiation table.

While it would be desirable to do venture capital deals with a simple agreement on price, a handshake, and a short legal agreement, this rarely happens. And while there have been plenty of attempts to standardize the term sheet over the years, the proliferation of lawyers, venture capitalists, and entrepreneurs, along with a steadily increasing number of investments, has prevented this from happening. Ironically, the actual definitive documents have become more standard over time. Whether it is the Internet age that has spread information across the ecosystem or clients growing tired of paying legal bills, there are more similarities in the documents today than ever before. As a result, we can lend you our experience in how venture financings are usually done. The good news is once you've negotiated the term sheet, you are done with the hard part. As a result, that's where we are going to focus our energy in this book.

Let's begin our exploration of venture capital financings by discussing the various players involved.

CHAPTER

1

The Players

While it might seem like there are only two players in the financing dance—the entrepreneur and the venture capitalist—there are often others, including angel investors, lawyers, and mentors. Any entrepreneur who has created a company that has gone through multiple financings knows that the number of people involved can quickly spiral out of control, especially if you aren't sure who actually is making the decisions at each step along the way.

The experience, motivation, and relative power of each participant in a financing can be complex, and the implications are often mysterious. Let's begin our journey to understanding venture capital financings by making sure we understand each player and the dynamics surrounding the participants.

The Entrepreneur

Not all investors realize it, but the entrepreneur is the center of the entrepreneurial universe. Without entrepreneurs there would be no term sheet and no startup ecosystem.

Throughout this book we use the words *entrepreneur* and *founder* interchangeably. While some companies have only one founder, many have two, three, or even more. Sometimes these co-founders are equals; other times they aren't. Regardless of the number, they each have a key role in the formation of the company and any financing that occurs.

The founders can't and shouldn't outsource their involvement in a financing to their lawyers. There are many issues in a financing negotiation that only the entrepreneurs can resolve. Even if you hire a fantastic lawyer who knows everything, don't forget that if your lawyer and your future investors don't get along you will have larger issues to deal with. If you are the entrepreneur, make sure you direct and control the process.

The relationship between the founders at the beginning of the life of a company is almost always good. If it's not, the term sheet and corresponding financing are probably the least of the founders' worries. However, as time passes, the relationship between co-founders often frays. This could be due to many different factors: the stress of the business, competence, personality, or even changing life priorities like a new spouse or children.

When this happens, one or more founders will often leave the business—sometimes on good terms and sometimes on not such good terms. Some investors know that it's best to anticipate these kinds of issues up front and will try to structure terms that predefine how things will work in these situations. The investors are often trying to protect the founders from each other by making sure things can be cleanly resolved without disrupting the company more than the departure of a founder already does.

We cover this dynamic in terms like vesting, drag-along rights, and co-sale rights. When we do, we discuss both the investor perspective and the entrepreneur perspective. You'll see this through the book—we've walked in both the investor's and the entrepreneur's shoes, and we try hard to take a balanced approach to our commentary.

The Venture Capitalist

The *venture capitalist* (VC) is the next character in the term sheet play. VCs come in many shapes, sizes, and experience levels. While most (but not all) profess to be entrepreneur-friendly, many fall far short of their aspirations. The first signs of this often appear during the term sheet negotiation.

Venture capital firms have their own hierarchies that are important for an entrepreneur to understand. Later in the book we'll dive into all the deep, dark secrets about how VCs are motivated and paid, and what their incentives can be. For now, we'll consider VCs as humans and talk about the people.

The most senior person in the firm is usually called a *managing director* (MD) or a *general partner* (GP). In some cases, these titles have an additional prefix—such as *executive managing director* or *founding general partner*—to signify even more seniority over the other managing directors or general partners. These VCs make the final investment decisions and sit on the boards of directors of the companies they invest in.

Principals, or *directors*, are usually next in line. These are junior deal partners—they are working their way up the ladder to managing director. Principals usually have some deal responsibility, but they almost always require support from a managing director to move a deal through the VC firm. So, while the principal has some power, he probably can't make a final decision.

Associates are typically not deal partners. Instead, they work directly for one or more deal partners, usually a managing director. Associates do a wide variety of things, including scouting for new deals, helping with due diligence on existing deals, and writing up endless internal memos about prospective investments. They are also likely to be the person in the firm who spends the most time with the *capitalization table* (also known as a *cap table*), which is the spreadsheet that defines the economics of the deal. Many firms have an associate program, usually lasting two years, after which time the associate leaves the firm to go work for a portfolio company, to go to business school, or to start up a company. Occasionally the star associates go on to become principals.

Analysts are at the bottom of the ladder. These are very junior people, usually recently graduated from college, who sit in a room with no windows down the hall from everyone else, crunch numbers, and write memos. In some firms, analysts and associates play similar roles and have similar functions; in others, the associates are more deal-centric. Regardless, analysts are generally smart people who are usually very limited in power and responsibility.

Some firms, especially larger ones, have a variety of *venture partners* or *operating partners*. These are usually experienced entrepreneurs who have a part-time relationship with the VC firm. While they have the ability to sponsor a deal, they often need explicit support of one of the managing directors, just as a principal would, in order to get a deal done. In some firms, operating partners don't sponsor deals, but take an active role in managing the investment as a chairman or board member.

Entrepreneurs in residence (EIRs) are another type of part-time member of the VC firm. EIRs are experienced entrepreneurs who park themselves at a VC firm while they are working on figuring out their next company. They often help the VC with introductions, due diligence, and networking during the three- to 12-month period that they are an EIR. Some VCs pay their EIRs; others simply provide them with free office space and an implicit agreement to invest in their next company.

In small firms, you might be dealing only with managing directors. For example, in our firm, Foundry Group, we have a total of four partners, all called managing directors, each of whom has the same responsibility, authority, and power. In large firms, you'll be dealing with a wide array of managing directors, principals, associates, analysts, venture partners, operating partners, EIRs, and other titles.

Entrepreneurs should do their research on the firms they are talking to in order to understand who they are talking to, what decision-making power that person has, and what process they have to go through to get an investment approved. The best source for this kind of information is other entrepreneurs who have worked with the VC firm in the past, although you'd also be surprised how much of this you can piece together just by looking at how the VC firm presents itself on its web site. If all else fails, you can always ask the VC how things work, although the further down the hierarchy of the firm, the less likely you'll get completely accurate information.

The Entrepreneur's Perspective

Managing directors or general partners have the mojo inside venture capital firms. If you have anyone else prospecting you or working on the deal with you (associate, senior associate, principal, venture partner, or EIR), treat him with an enormous amount of respect, but insist on developing a direct relationship with an MD or a GP as well. Anyone other than an MD or a GP is unlikely to be at the firm for the long haul. The MDs and GPs are the ones who matter and who will make decisions about your company.

The Angel Investor

In addition to VCs, your investor group may include individual investors, usually referred to as *angel investors* (or *angel* for short). These angels are often a key source of early stage investment and are very active in the first round of investment, or the *seed stage*. Angels can be professional investors, successful entrepreneurs, friends, or family members.

Many VCs are very comfortable investing along with angels and often encourage their active involvement early in the life of a company. As a result, the angels are an important part of any financing dance. However, not all angels are created equal, nor do all VCs share the same view of angels.

While angels will invest at various points in time, they usually invest in the early rounds and often don't participate in future rounds. In cases where everything is going well, this is rarely an issue. However, if the company hits some speed bumps and has a difficult financing, the angels' participation in future rounds may come into question. Some of the terms we discuss in the book, such as *pay-to-play* and *drag-along rights*, are specifically designed to help the VCs force a certain type of behavior on the angels (and other VC investors) in these difficult financing rounds.

While angel investors are usually high-net-worth individuals, they aren't always. There are specific SEC rules around *accredited investors* and you should make sure that each of your angel investors qualifies as an accredited investor or has an appropriate exemption. The best way to ensure this is to ask your lawyer for help on the rules.

Some angel investors make a lot of small investments. Recently, these very active, or promiscuous, angels have started to be called *super angels*. These super angels are often experienced entrepreneurs who have had one or more exits and have decided to invest their own money in new startups. In most cases, super angels are well known in entrepreneurial circles and are often a huge help to early stage companies.

As super angels make more investments, they often decide to raise capital from their friends, other entrepreneurs, or institutions. At this point the super angel raises a fund similar to a *VC fund* and has actually become an institutionalized super angel, which is starting to be known as a *micro VC*. While these micro VCs often want to be thought of as angels instead of VCs, once they've raised money from other people they have the same fiduciary responsibility to their investors that a VC has, and as a result they are really just VCs.

It's important to remember that there isn't a generic angel investor type (nor is there a generic VC type). Lumping them together and referring to them as a single group can be dangerous. Never assume any of these people are like one another. They will all have their own incentives, pressures, experiences, and sophistication levels. Their individual characteristics will often define your working relationship with them well beyond any terms that you negotiate.

The Entrepreneur's Perspective

Don't put yourself in a position where you can be held hostage by angels. They are important, but they are rarely in a position to determine the company's direction. If your angel group is a small, diffuse list of friends and family, consider setting up a special-purpose limited partnership controlled by one of them as a vehicle for them to invest. Chasing down 75 signatures when you want to do a financing or sell the company is not fun.

Also, true friends and family need special care. Make sure they understand up front that (1) they should think of their investment as a lottery ticket, and (2) every time they see you at a holiday or birthday party is not an investor relations meeting.

The Syndicate

While some VCs invest alone, many invest with other VCs. A collection of investors is called a *syndicate*.

When VCs refer to the syndicate, they are often talking about the major participants in the financing round, which are usually but not always VCs. The syndicate includes any investor, whether a VC, angel, super angel, strategic investor, corporation, law firm, or anyone else that ends up purchasing equity in the financing.

Most syndicates have a *lead investor*. Usually, but not always, this is one of the VC investors. Two VCs will often co-lead a syndicate, and occasionally you'll see three co-leads.

While there is nothing magical about who the lead investor is, having one often makes it easier for the entrepreneurs to focus their energy around the negotiation. Rather than having one-off negotiations with each investor, the lead in the syndicate will often take the role of negotiating terms for the entire syndicate.

Regardless of the lead investor or the structure of the syndicate, it is the entrepreneurs' responsibility to make sure they are communicating with each of the investors in the syndicate. As the entrepreneur, even though the lead investor may help corral the other investors through the process, don't assume that you don't need to communicate with each of the investors—you do!

> ### The Entrepreneur's Perspective
>
> While you should communicate with all investors, you should insist that investors agree (at least verbally) that the lead investor can speak for the whole syndicate when it comes to investment terms. You should not let yourself be in a position where you have to negotiate the same deal multiple times. If there is dissension in the ranks, ask the lead investor for help.

The Lawyer

Ah, the lawyers—I bet you thought we'd never get to them. In deals, a great lawyer can be a huge help and a bad lawyer can be a disaster.

For the entrepreneur, an experienced lawyer who understands VC financings is invaluable. VCs make investments all the time. Entrepreneurs raise money occasionally. Even a very experienced entrepreneur runs the risk of getting hung up on a nuance that a VC has thought through many times.

In addition to helping negotiate, a great lawyer can help focus the entrepreneur on what really matters. While this book will cover all the terms that typically come up in a VC financing, we'll continue to repeat a simple mantra that the real terms that matter are economics and control. Yes, VCs will inevitably spend time negotiating for an additional S-3 registration right (an unimportant term that we'll discuss later) even though the chance it ever comes into play is very slight. This is just life in a negotiation—there are always endless tussles over unimportant points, sometimes due to silly reasons, but they are often used as a negotiating strategy to distract you from the main show. VCs are experts at this; a great lawyer can keep you from falling into these traps.

However, a bad lawyer, or one inexperienced in VC financings, can do you a world of harm. In addition to getting outnegotiated, the inexperienced lawyer will focus on the wrong issues, fight hard on things that don't matter, and run up the bill on both sides. We've encountered this numerous times. Whenever entrepreneurs want to use their cousin who is a divorce lawyer, we take an aggressive position before we start negotiating that the entrepreneur needs a lawyer who has a clue.

Never forget that your lawyer is a reflection on you. Your reputation in the startup ecosystem is important, and a bad or inexperienced lawyer will tarnish it. Furthermore, once the deal is done, you'll be partners with your investors; so you don't want a bad or inexperienced lawyer creating unnecessary tension in the financing negotiation that will carry over once you are partners with your investors.

The Entrepreneur's Perspective

At the same time that you don't want an inexperienced lawyer creating unnecessary tension in the negotiation, don't let a VC talk you out of using your lawyer of choice just because that lawyer isn't from a nationally known firm or the lawyer rubs the VC the wrong way. This is *your* lawyer, not your VC's lawyer. That said, to do this well, you need to be close enough to the communication to make sure your lawyer is being reasonable and communicating clearly and in a friendly manner.

While lawyers usually bill by the hour, many lawyers experienced with VC investments will cap their fees in advance of the deal. As of this writing in 2012, a very early stage financing can be done for between $5,000 and $15,000 and a typical financing can be completed for between $25,000 and $40,000. Lawyers in large cities tend to charge more, and if your company has any items to clean up from your past, your costs will increase.

If your lawyers and the VC lawyers don't get along, your bill can skyrocket if you don't stay involved in the process. If the lawyers are unwilling to agree to a modest fee cap, you should question whether they know what they are doing.

In case you are curious, these numbers are virtually unchanged from a decade ago while billable rates have more than doubled in the same time. What this means is that document standardization is a reality, but it also means that the average lawyer spends less time per deal than in ancient times (the 1990s). Once again, the entrepreneur must take responsibility for the final results.

> ### The Entrepreneur's Perspective
>
> Don't be shy about insisting that your lawyer take a lower cap or even that the lawyer will only get paid out of the proceeds of a deal. There's no reason, if you are a solid entrepreneur with a good business, that even a top-tier law firm won't take your unpaid deal to its executive committee as a flier to be paid on closing.

The Mentor

Every entrepreneur should have a stable of experienced *mentors*. These mentors can be hugely useful in any financing, especially if they know the VCs involved.

We like to refer to these folks as mentors instead of advisers since the word *adviser* often implies that there is some sort of fee agreement with the company. It's unusual for a company, especially an early stage one, to have a fee arrangement with an adviser around a financing. Nonetheless, there are advisers who prey on entrepreneurs by showing up, offering to help raise money, and then asking for compensation by taking a cut of the deal. There are even some bold advisers who ask for a retainer relationship to help out. We encourage early stage entrepreneurs to stay away from these advisers.

In contrast, mentors help the entrepreneurs, especially early stage ones, because someone once helped them. Many mentors end up being early angel investors in companies or get a small equity grant for serving on the board of directors or board of advisers, but they rarely ask for anything up front.

While having mentors is never required, we strongly encourage entrepreneurs to find them, work with them, and build long-term relationships with them. The benefits are enormous and often surprising. Most great mentors we know do it because they enjoy it. When this is the motivation, you often see some great relationships develop.

The Entrepreneur's Perspective

Mentors are great. There's no reason not to give someone a small success fee if they truly help you raise money (random email introductions to a VC they met once at a cocktail party don't count). Sometimes it will make sense to compensate mentors with options as long as you have some control over the vesting of the options based on your satisfaction with the mentor's performance as an ongoing adviser.

How to Raise Money

Your goal when you are raising a round of financing should be to get several term sheets. While we have plenty of suggestions, there is no single way to do this, as financings come together in lots of different ways. VCs are not a homogeneous group; what might impress one VC might turn off another. Although we know what works for us and for our firm, each firm is different; so make sure you know who you are dealing with, what their approach is, and what kind of material they need during the fund-raising process. Following are some basic but by no means complete rules of the road, along with some things that you shouldn't do.

Do or Do Not; There Is No Try

In addition to being a small, green, hairy puppet, Yoda was a wise man. His seminal statement to young Luke Skywalker is one we believe every entrepreneur should internalize before hitting the fund-raising trail. You must have the mind-set that you will succeed on your quest.

When we meet people who say they are "trying to raise money," "testing the waters," or "exploring different options," this not only is a turnoff, but also often shows they've not had much success. Start with an attitude of presuming success. If you don't, investors will smell this uncertainty on you; it'll permeate your words and actions.

Not all entrepreneurs will succeed when they go out to raise a financing. Failure is a key part of entrepreneurship, but, as with many things in life, attitude impacts outcome and this is one of those cases.

Determine How Much You Are Raising

Before you hit the road, figure out how much money you are going to raise. This will impact your choice of those you speak to in the process. For instance, if you are raising a $500,000 seed round, you'll talk to angel investors, seed stage VCs, super angels, micro VCs, and early stage investors, including ones from very large VC funds. However, if you are going out to raise $10 million, you should start with larger VC firms since you'll need a lead investor who can write at least a $5 million check.

While you can create complex financial models that determine that you need a specific amount of capital down to the penny to become cash flow positive, we know one thing with 100 percent certainty: these models will be wrong. Instead, focus on a length of time you want to fund your company to get to the next meaningful milestone. If you are just starting out, how long will it take you to ship your first product? Or, if you have a product in the market, how long will it take to get to a certain number of users or a specific revenue amount? Then, assume no revenue growth; what is the monthly spend (or total burn rate) that you need to get to this point? If you are starting out and think it'll take six months to get a product to market with a team of eight people, you can quickly estimate that you'll spend around $100,000 per month for six months. Give yourself some time cushion (say, a year) and raise $1 million, since it'll take you a few months to ramp up to a $100,000-per-month burn rate.

The length of time you need varies dramatically by business. In a seed stage software company, you should be able to make real progress in around a year. If you are trying to get a drug approved by the Food and Drug Administration (FDA), you'll need at least several years. Don't obsess about getting this exactly right—as with your financial model, it's likely wrong (or approximate at best). Just make sure you have enough cash to get to a clear point of demonstrable success. That said, be careful not to overspecify the milestones that you are going to achieve—you don't want them showing up in your financing documents as specific milestones that you have to attain.

Be careful not to go out asking for an amount that is larger than you need, since one of the worst positions you can be in during a financing is to have investors interested, but be too far short of your goal. For example, assume you are a seed stage company that needs $500,000 but you go out looking for $1 million. One of the questions that the VCs and angels you meet with will probably ask you is: "How much money do you have committed to the round?" If you answer with "I have $250,000 committed," a typical angel may feel you're never going to get there and will hold back on engaging just based on the status of your financing. However, being able to say "I'm at $400,000 on a $500,000 raise and we've got room for one or two more investors" is a powerful statement to a prospective angel investor since most investors love to be part of an oversubscribed round.

Finally, we don't believe in ranges in the fund-raising process. When someone says they are raising $5 million to $7 million, our first question is: "Is it $5 million or $7 million?" Though it might feel comfortable to offer up a range in case you can't get to the high end of it, presumably you want to raise at least the low number. The range makes it appear like you are hedging your bets or that you haven't thought hard about how much money you actually need to raise. Instead, we always recommend stating that you are raising a specific number, and then, when you have more investor demand than you can handle, you can always raise more.

Fund-Raising Materials

While the exact fund-raising materials you will need can vary widely by VC, there are a few basic things that you should create before you hit the fund-raising trail. At the minimum, you need a short description of your business, an *executive summary*, and a presentation that is often not so fondly referred to as "a PowerPoint." Some investors will ask for a business plan or a *private placement memorandum* (PPM); this is more common in later stage investments.

Once upon a time, physical form seemed to matter. In the 1980s, elaborate business plans were professionally printed at the corner copy shop and mailed out. Today, virtually all materials are sent via email. Quality still matters a lot, but it's usually in substance with appropriate form. Don't overdesign your information—we can't tell you the number of times we've gotten a highly stylized executive summary that was organized in such a way as to be visually appealing, yet completely lacking in substance. Focus on the content while making the presentation solid.

Finally, while never required, many investors (such as us) respond to things we can play with, so even if you are a very early stage company, a prototype, or demo is desirable.

Short Description of Your Business

You'll need a few paragraphs that you can email, often called the *elevator pitch*, meaning you should be able to give it during the length of time it takes for an elevator to go from the first floor to your prospective investor's office. Don't confuse this with the executive summary, which we discuss next; rather, this is between one and three paragraphs that describe the product, the team, and the business very directly. It doesn't need to be a separate document that you attach to an email; this is the bulk of the email, often wrapped with an introductory paragraph, especially if you know the person or are being referred to the person, and a concluding paragraph with a very clear request for whatever next step you want.

Executive Summary

The executive summary is a one- to three-page description of your idea, product, team, and business. It's a short, concise, well-written document that is the first substantive document and interaction you'll likely have with a prospective investor with whom you don't have a preexisting relationship. Think of the executive summary as the basis for your first impression, and expect it to be passed around within a VC firm if there's any interest in what you are doing.

Work hard on the executive summary—the more substance you can pack into this short document, the more a VC will believe that you have thought critically about your business. It also is a direct indication of your communication skills. A poorly written summary that leaves out key pieces of information will cause the VC to assume that you haven't thought deeply about some important issues or that you are trying to hide bad facts about the business.

In the summary, include the problem you are solving and why it's important to solve. Explain why your product is awesome, why it's better than what currently exists, and why your team is the right one to pursue it. End with some high-level financial data to show that you have aggressive, but sensible expectations about how your business will perform over time.

Your first communication with a VC is often an introductory email, either from you or from someone referring you to the VC, that is a combination of the short description of your business along with the executive summary attached to the email. If your first interaction was a face-to-face meeting either at a conference, at a coffee shop, or in an elevator, if a VC is interested he'll often say something like "Can you send me an executive summary?" Do this the same day that it is requested of you to start to build momentum to the next step in the process.

Presentation

Once you've engaged with a VC firm, you'll quickly be asked either to give or to email a presentation. This is usually a 10- to 20-page Power-Point presentation consisting of a substantive overview of your business. There are many different presentation styles and approaches, and what you need will depend on the audience (one person, a VC partnership, or 500 people at an investor day type of event). Your goal with the presentation is to communicate the same information as the executive summary, but using a visual presentation.

Over time, a number of different presentation styles have emerged. A three-minute presentation at a local pitch event is just as different from an eight-minute presentation at an *accelerator*'s investor day as it is from a 30-minute presentation to a VC partnership. Recognize your audience and tune your presentation to them. Realize also that the deck you email as an overview can be different from the one you present, even if you are covering similar material.

Regardless, spend time on the presentation flow and format. In this case, form matters a great deal—it's amazing how much more positive a response is to well-designed and well-organized slides, especially if you have a consumer-facing product where user experience will matter a lot for its success. If you don't have a good designer on your team, find a friend who is a freelance designer to help you turn your presentation into something visually appealing. It will pay off many times over.

The Entrepreneur's Perspective

"Less is more" when it comes to an investor presentation. There are only a few key things most VCs look at to understand and get excited about a deal: the problem you are solving, the size of the opportunity, the strength of the team, the level of competition or competitive advantage that you have, your plan of attack, and current status. Summary financials, use of proceeds, and milestones are also important. Most good investor presentations can be done in 10 slides or fewer.

Business Plan

We haven't read a business plan in over 20 years. Sure, we still get plenty of them, but it is not something we care about as we invest in areas we know well, and as a result we much prefer demos and live interactions. Fortunately, most business plans arrive in email these days, so they are easy enough to ignore since one doesn't have to physically touch them. However, realize that some VCs care a lot about seeing a business plan, regardless of the current view by many people that a business plan is an obsolete document.

The business plan is usually a 30-ish-page document that has all sorts of sections and is something you would learn to write if you went to business school. It goes into great detail about all facets of the business, expanding on the executive summary to have comprehensive sections about the market, product, target customer, go-to-market strategy, team, and financials.

While we think business plans prepared specifically for fundraising are a waste of time, we still believe that they are a valuable document for entrepreneurs to write while they are formulating their business. There are lots of different approaches today, including many that are user- or customer-centric, but the discipline of writing down what you are thinking, your hypotheses about your business, and what you believe will happen is still very useful.

Now, we aren't talking about a conventional business plan, although this can be a useful approach. Rather, if you are a software company, consider some variant of the Lean Startup methodology that includes the creation, launch, and testing of a minimum viable product as a starting point. Or, rather than writing an extensive document, use PowerPoint to organize your thoughts into clear sections, although recognize this is very different from the presentation you are going to give potential investors.

Regardless, you will occasionally be asked for a business plan. Be prepared for this and know how you plan to respond, along with what you will provide, if and when this comes up.

Private Placement Memorandum

A private placement memorandum (PPM) is essentially a traditional business plan wrapped in legal disclaimers that are often as long as the plan itself is. It's time-consuming and expensive to prepare, and you get the privilege of paying lawyers thousands of dollars to proofread the document and provide a bunch of legal boilerplate to ensure you don't say anything that you could get sued for later.

Normally PPMs are generated only when investment bankers are involved and are fund-raising from large entities and banks that demand a PPM. That being said, we've seen plenty of early stage companies hire bankers and draft PPMs. To us, this is a waste of money and time. When we see an email from a banker sending us a PPM for an early stage company, we automatically know that investment opportunity isn't for us and almost always toss it in the circular file.

Our view is that if an early stage company has hired a banker to help with fund-raising, either it has been unsuccessful in its attempt to raise money and is hoping the banker can help it in a last-ditch effort or it is getting bad advice from its advisers (who may be the ones making a fee from marketing the deal via the PPM). While many later stage investors like to look at all the stuff they get from investment bankers, we generally think this is a pretty weak approach for an early stage company.

Detailed Financial Model

The only thing that we know about financial predictions of startups is that 100 percent of them are wrong. If you can predict the future accurately, we have a few suggestions for other things you could be doing besides starting a risky early stage company. Furthermore, the earlier stage the startup, the less accurate any predications will be. While we know you can't predict your revenue with any degree of accuracy (although we are always very pleased in that rare case where revenue starts earlier and grows faster than expected), the expense side of your financial plan is very instructive as to how you think about the business.

You can't predict your revenue with any level of precision, but you should be able to manage your expenses exactly to plan. Your financials will mean different things to different investors. In our case, we focus on two things: (1) the assumptions underlying the revenue forecast (which we don't need a spreadsheet for—we'd rather just talk about them) and (2) the monthly burn rate or cash consumption of the business. Since your revenue forecast will be wrong, your cash flow forecast will be wrong. However, if you are an effective manager, you'll know how to budget for this by focusing on lagging your increase in cash spend behind your expected growth in revenue.

Other VCs are much more spreadsheet driven. Some firms (usually those with associates) may go so far as to perform discounted cash flow analysis to determine the value of your business. Some will look at every line item and study it in detail. Others will focus much less on all the details, but focus on certain things that matter to them. For instance, what is your head count over the next few quarters and how fast do you expect to acquire users/customers? Although none of us know your business better than you do, VCs are in the business of pattern recognition and will apply their experience and frame of reference to your financial model as they evaluate how well you understand the financial dynamics of your business.

The Demo

Most VCs love demos. In the 48 hours before we wrote this section we got to play with an industrial robot, wear a device that tracked our anxiety level, interact with software that measured the number of times we smiled while we watched a video, saw a projection system that worked on curved walls with incredible fidelity, and played around with a Web service that figured out the news we were interested in based on a new approach to leveraging our social graphs. We learned more from the demos, especially about our emotional interest in the products we played with, than any document could communicate. Each of these demos also gave us a chance to talk directly to the entrepreneurs about how they thought about their current and future products, and we got a clear read of the enthusiasm and passion of the entrepreneurs for what they are working on.

We believe the demo, a prototype, or an alpha is far more important than a business plan or financial model for a very early stage company. The demo shows us your vision in a way we can interact with. More important, it shows us that you can build something and then show it off. We expect demos to be underfeatured, to be rough around the edges, and to crash. We know that you'll probably throw away the demo on the way to a final product and what we are investing in will evolve a lot. But, like 14-year-old boys, we just want to play.

Demos are just as important in existing companies. If you have a complex product, figure out a way to show it off in a short period of time. We don't need to see every feature; use your demo to tell us a story about the problem your product addresses. And give us the steering wheel—we want to play with the demo, not just be passive observers. While we are playing, watch us carefully because you'll learn an enormous amount about us in that brief period of time while you see how comfortable we are, whether our eyes light up, and whether we really understand what you are pursuing.

Due Diligence Materials

As you go further down the financing path, VCs will ask for additional information. If a VC firm offers you a term sheet, expect its lawyers to ask you for a bunch of things such as capitalization tables, contracts and material agreements, employment agreements, and board meeting minutes. The list of documents requested during the formal due diligence process (usually after signing of the term sheet, but not always) can be long. For an example, see the "Resources" page on AsktheVC.com. The number of documents you will actually have will depend on how long you have been in business. Even if you are a young company just starting up, we recommend that before you go out to raise money you organize all of these documents for quick delivery to a potential funding partner so you don't slow down the process when they ask for them.

Keep in mind that you should never try to hide anything with any of these fund-raising materials. Although you are trying to present your company in the best light possible, you want to make sure any issues you have are clearly disclosed. Deal with any messy stuff up front, and if a VC forgets to ask for something early on, assume you will be asked for it before the deal is done. If you happen to get something past a VC and get funded, it will eventually come out that you weren't completely transparent and your relationship will suffer. A good VC will respect full disclosure early on and, if they are interested in working with you, will actively engage to help you get through any challenges you have, or at least give you feedback on why there are showstoppers that you have to clear up before you raise money.

Finding the Right VC

The best way to find the perfect VC is to ask your friends and other entrepreneurs. They can give you unfiltered data about which

VCs they've enjoyed working with and who have helped build their businesses. It's also the most efficient approach, since an introduction to a VC from an entrepreneur who knows both you and the VC is always more effective than you sending a cold email to vcname@vcfirm.com.

But what should you do if you don't have a large network for this? Back in the early days of venture capital, it was very hard to locate even the contact information for a VC and you rarely found them in the yellow pages, not even next to the folks that give payday loans. Today, VCs have web sites, blog, tweet endlessly, and even list their email addresses on their web sites.

Entrepreneurs can discover a lot of information about their potential future VC partner well beyond the mundane contact information. You'll be able to discover what types of companies they invest in, what stage of growth they prefer to invest in, past successes, failures, approaches and strategies (at least their marketing approach), and bios on the key personnel at the firm.

If the VC has a social media presence, you'll be able to take all of that information and infer things like their hobbies, theories on investing, beer they drink, instrument they play, and type of building or facility—such as a bathroom—they like to endow at their local universities. If you follow them on Foursquare, you can even figure out what kind of food they like to eat.

While it may seem obvious, engaging a VC that you don't know via social media can be useful as a starting point to develop a relationship. In addition to the ego gratification of having a lot of Twitter followers, you'll start to develop an impression and, more important, a relationship if you comment thoughtfully on blog posts the VC writes. It doesn't have to be all business—engage at a personal level, offer suggestions, interact, and follow the best rule of developing relationships, which is to "give more than you get." And never forget the simple notion that if you want money, ask for advice.

Do your homework. When we get business plans from medical tech companies or somebody insisting we sign a nondisclosure agreement (NDA) before we review a business plan, we know that they did absolutely zero research on our firm or us before they sent us the information. At best, the submission doesn't rise to the top compared to more thoughtful correspondences, and at worst it doesn't even elicit a response from us.

A typical VC gets thousands of inquiries a year. The vast majority of these requests are from people that the VC has never met and with whom the VC has no relationship. Improve your chances of having VCs respond to you by researching them, getting a referral to them, and engaging with them in whatever way they seem to be interested in.

Finally, don't forget this works both ways. You may have a super-hot deal and as a result have your pick of VCs to fund your company. Do your homework and find out who will be most helpful to your success, has a temperament and style that will be compatible with yours, and will ultimately be your best long-term partner.

Finding a Lead VC

Assuming that you are talking with multiple potential investors, you can generally categorize them into one of three groups: leaders, followers, and everyone else. It's important to know how to interact with each of these groups. If not, you not only will waste a lot of your time, but also might be unsuccessful in your fund-raising mission.

Your goal is to find a lead VC. This is the firm that is going to put down the term sheet, take a leadership role in driving to a financing, and likely be your most active new investor. It's possible to have co-leads (usually two, occasionally three) in a financing. It's also desirable to have more than one lead VC competing to lead your deal, without them knowing whom else you are talking to.

As you meet with potential VCs, you'll get one of four typical vibes. First is the VC who clearly is interested and wants to lead. Next is the VC who isn't interested and passes. These are the easy ones—engage aggressively with the ones who want to lead and don't worry about the ones who pass.

The other two categories—the "maybe" and the "slow no"—are the hardest to deal with. The "maybe" seems interested, but doesn't really step up his level of engagement. This VC seems to be hanging around, waiting to see if there's any interest in your deal. Keep this person warm by continually meeting and communicating with him, but realize that this VC is not going to catalyze your investment. However, as your deal comes together with a lead, this VC is a great one to bring into the mix if you want to put a syndicate of several firms together.

The "slow no" is the hardest to figure out. These VCs never actually say no, but are completely in react mode. They'll occasionally respond when you reach out to them, but there is no perceived forward motion on their part. You always feel like you are pushing on a rope—there's a little resistance but nothing ever really moves anywhere. We recommend you think of these VCs as a "no" and don't continue to spend time with them.

How VCs Decide to Invest

Let's explore how VCs decide to invest in a company and what the process normally looks like. All VCs are different, so these are generalizations, but more or less reflect the way that VCs make their decisions.

The way that you get connected to a particular VC affects the process that you go through. Some VCs will fund only entrepreneurs with whom they have a prior connection. Other VCs prefer to be introduced to entrepreneurs by other VCs. Some VCs invest only in seasoned entrepreneurs and avoid working with first-time entrepreneurs, whereas others, like us, will fund entrepreneurs of all ages and experience and will try to be responsive to anyone who contacts us. Whatever the case is, you should determine quickly if you reached a particular VC through his preferred channel or you are swimming upstream from the beginning.

Next, you should understand the role of the person within the VC firm who is your primary connection. If an associate reached out to you via email, consider that his job is to scour the universe looking for deals, but that the associate probably doesn't have any real pull to get a deal done. It doesn't mean that you shouldn't meet with him, but also don't get overly excited until there is a general partner or managing director at the firm paying attention to and spending real time with you.

Your first few interactions with a VC firm will vary widely depending on the firm's style and who your initial contact is. However, at some point it will be apparent that the VC has more than a passing interest in exploring an investment in you and will begin a process often known as *due diligence*. This isn't a formal legal or technical diligence; rather it's code for "I'm taking my exploration to the next level."

You can learn a lot about the attitude and culture of a VC firm by the way it conducts its diligence. For example, if you are raising your first round of financing and you have no revenue and no product, a VC who asks for a five-year detailed financial projection and then proceeds to hammer you on the numbers is probably not someone who has a lot of experience or comfort making early stage investments. As mentioned before, we believe the only thing that can be known about a prerevenue company's financial projections is that they are wrong.

During this phase, a VC will ask for a lot of things, such as presentations, projections, customer pipeline or targets, development plan, competitive analysis, and team bios. This is all normal. In some cases the VCs will be mellow and accept what you've already created in anticipation of the financing. In other cases, they'll make you run around like a headless chicken and create a lot of busywork for you. In either case, before you jump through hoops providing this information, again make sure a partner-level person (usually a managing director or general partner) is involved and that you aren't just the object of a fishing expedition by an associate.

The Entrepreneur's Perspective

If you feel like your VC is a proctologist, run for the hills.

While the VC firm goes through its diligence process on you, we suggest you return the favor and ask for things like introductions to other founders they've backed. Nothing is as illuminating as a discussion with other entrepreneurs who've worked with your potential investor. Don't be afraid to ask for entrepreneurs the VC has backed whose companies haven't worked out. Since you should expect that a good VC will ask around about you, don't be afraid to ask other entrepreneurs what they think of the VC.

The Entrepreneur's Perspective

The best VCs will give you, either proactively or reactively, a list of all the entrepreneurs they've worked with in the past and ask you to pick a few for reference checks. The best reference checks are ones you can do where the company went through hard times, maybe swapped out a founder for another CEO, or even failed, as you will learn from these how the VC handled messy and adversarial situations.

You'll go through multiple meetings, emails, phone calls, and more meetings. You may meet other members of the firm or you may not. You may end up going to the VC's offices to present to the entire partnership on a Monday, a tradition known by many firms as the Monday partner meeting. In other cases, as with our firm, if things are heating up you'll meet with each of the partners relatively early in the process in one-on-one or group settings.

As the process unfolds, either you'll continue to work with the VC in exploring the opportunity or the VC will start slowing down the pace of communication. Be very wary of the VC who is hot on your company, then warm, then cold, but never really says no. While some VCs are quick to say no when they lose interest, many VCs don't say no because either they don't see a reason to, they want to keep their options open, they are unwilling to affirmatively pass on a deal because they don't want to have to shut the door, or they are just plain impolite and disrespectful to the entrepreneur.

Ultimately VCs will decide to invest or not invest. If they do, the next step in the process is for them to issue a term sheet.

The Entrepreneur's Perspective

If a VC passes on a deal with you, whether graciously or by not returning your emails and your calls, do your best to politely insist on feedback as to why. This is one of the most important lessons an entrepreneur can learn and is especially useful during the fund-raising cycle. Don't worry that someone is telling you that your baby is ugly. Ask for the feedback, demand it, get it, absorb it, and learn from it.

Closing the Deal

The most important part of all of the fund-raising process is to close the deal, raise the money, and get back to running your business. How do you actually close the deal?

Separate it into two activities: the first is the signing of the term sheet and the second is signing the definitive documents and getting the cash. This book is primarily about getting a term sheet signed. In our experience, most executed term sheets result in a financing that closes. Reputable VCs can't afford to have term sheets signed and then not follow through; otherwise they don't remain reputable for long.

The most likely situations that derail financings are when VCs find unexpected bad facts about the company after term sheet signing. You should assume that a signed term sheet will lead to money in the bank as long as there are no smoking guns in your company's past, the investor is a professional one, and you don't do anything stupid in the definitive document drafting process.

The second part of closing the deal is the process of drafting the definitive agreements. Generally, the lawyers do most of the heavy lifting here. They will take the term sheet and start to negotiate the 100-plus pages of documentation that are generated from the term sheet. In the best-case scenario, you respond to due diligence requests and one day you are told to sign some documents. The next thing you know, you have money in the bank and a new board member you are excited to work with.

In the worst case, however, the deal blows up. Or perhaps the deal closes, but there are hard feelings left on both sides. As we restate in several parts of this book, always make sure that you are keeping tabs on the process. Don't let the lawyers behave poorly, as this will only injure the future relationship between you and your investor. Make sure that you are responsive with requests, and never assume that because your lawyer is angry and says the other side is horrible/stupid/evil/worthless that the VC even has a clue what is going on. Many times, we've seen the legal teams get completely tied up on an issue and want to kill each other when neither the entrepreneur nor the VC even cared about the issue or had any notion that there was a dustup over the issue. Before you get emotional, just place a simple phone call or send an email to the VC and see what the real story is.

Overview of the Term Sheet

At the end of 2005, we participated in a financing that was much more difficult than it needed to be. All of the participants were to blame, and ignorance of what really mattered in the negotiation kept things going much longer than was necessary. We talked about what to do and, at the risk of giving away super-top-secret VC magic tricks, decided to write a blog series on Brad's blog (Feld Thoughts—www.feld.com) that deconstructed a venture capital term sheet and explained each section.

That blog series was the inspiration for this book. The next few chapters cover the most frequently discussed terms in a VC term sheet. Many VCs love to negotiate hard on every term as though the health of their children depended on them getting the terms just right. Sometimes this is inexperience on the part of the VC; often it's just a negotiating tactic.

The specific language that we refer to is from actual term sheets. In addition to describing and explaining the specific terms, we give you examples of what to focus on and implications from the perspectives of the company, VCs, and entrepreneurs.

The Entrepreneur's Perspective

The term sheet is critical. What's in it usually determines the final deal structure. Don't think of it as a letter of intent. Think of it as a blueprint for your future relationship with your investor.

The Key Concepts: Economics and Control

In general, there are only two things that VCs really care about when making investments: economics and control. *Economics* refers to the return the investors will ultimately get in a liquidity event, usually either a sale of the company or an initial public offering (IPO), and the terms that have direct impact on this return. *Control* refers to the mechanisms that allow the investors either to affirmatively exercise control over the business or to veto certain decisions the company can make. If you are negotiating a deal and investors are digging their heels in on a provision that doesn't impact the economics or control, they are often blowing smoke, rather than elucidating substance.

The Entrepreneur's Perspective

Economics and control are important things to pay attention to, in and of themselves. They rule the day. An inexperienced VC will harp on other terms needlessly. You can give in on them or not, but the mere fact that a VC focuses on unimportant terms is a sign of what that VC will be like to work with as an owner, board member, and compensation committee member.

When companies are created, the founders receive *common stock*. However, when VCs invest in companies, they purchase *equity* and usually receive *preferred stock*. In the following chapters we'll be referring to terms that the preferred shareholders are receiving.

Separate financings are usually referred to as a series designated by a letter, such as *Series A*. The first round is often called the *Series A financing*, although recently a new round occurring before the Series A has appeared called the *Series Seed financing*. The letter is incremented in each subsequent financing, so Series B financings follow Series A, and Series C financings follow Series B. You'll occasionally see a number added onto the letter for subsequent rounds, such as Series A-1 or Series B-2. This is generally done to try to limit how far into the alphabet you go and is often used when the same investors do subsequent rounds in a company together. While we aren't aware of the world record for number of financings in a private company, we have seen a Series K financing.

In each of the following sections, we walk you through language for each term and detailed examples. Let's get started by exploring the economic terms.

Economic Terms of the Term Sheet

When discussing the economics of a VC deal, one often hears the question "What is the valuation?" While the valuation of a company, determined by multiplying the number of shares outstanding by the price per share, is one component of the deal, it's a mistake to focus only on the valuation when considering the economics of a deal.

In this chapter we discuss all of the terms that make up the economics of the deal, including price, liquidation preference, pay-to-play, vesting, the employee pool, and antidilution.

Price

The first economic term, and the one most entrepreneurs focus on more than any other, is the price of the deal. Following is the typical way price is represented in a term sheet.

> Price: $_____ per share (the Original Purchase Price). The Original Purchase Price represents a fully diluted premoney valuation of $ __ million and a fully diluted postmoney valuation of $__ million. For purposes of the above calculation and any other reference to fully diluted in this term sheet, fully diluted assumes the conversion of all outstanding preferred stock of the Company, the exercise of all authorized and currently existing stock options and warrants of the Company, and the increase of the Company's existing option pool by [X] shares prior to this financing.

A somewhat different way that price can be represented is by defining the amount of the financing, which backs into the price. For example:

> Amount of Financing: An aggregate of $X million, representing a __ percent ownership position on a fully diluted basis, including shares reserved for any employee option pool. Prior to the Closing, the Company will reserve shares of its Common Stock so that __ percent of its fully diluted capital stock following the issuance of its Series A Preferred is available for future issuances to directors, officers, employees, and consultants.

While *price per share* is the ultimate measure of what is being paid for the equity being bought, price is often referred to as *valuation*.

There are two different ways to discuss valuation: *premoney* and *postmoney*. The premoney valuation is what the investor is valuing the company at today, before investment, while the postmoney valuation is simply the premoney valuation plus the contemplated aggregate investment amount. With this, you've encountered the first trap that VCs often lead entrepreneurs into.

When a VC says, "I'll invest $5 million at a valuation of $20 million," the VC usually means the postmoney valuation. In this situation, the VC's expectation is that a $5 million investment will buy 25 percent of a $20 million postmoney company. At the same time, an entrepreneur might hear a $5 million investment at a *premoney* valuation of $20 million, which would buy only 20 percent of the $25 million postmoney company. The words are the same but the expectations are very different.

The term sheet language usually spells this out in detail. However, when you are starting the negotiation with the VC, you'll often have a verbal discussion about price. How you approach this sets the tone for a lot of the balance of the negotiation. By addressing the ambiguity up front, you demonstrate that you have knowledge about the basic terms. The best entrepreneurs we've dealt with are presumptive and say something like "I assume you mean $20 million premoney." This forces the VC to clarify, and if in fact he did mean $20 million premoney, it doesn't cost you anything in the negotiation.

The next part of price to focus on is the phrase *fully diluted*. Both the company and the investor will want to make sure the company has sufficient equity (or *stock options*) reserved to compensate and motivate its workforce. This is also known as the *employee pool* or *option pool*. The bigger the pool the better, right? Not so fast. Although a large option pool will make it less likely that the company will run out of available options, the size of the pool is taken into account in the valuation of the company, thereby effectively lowering the actual premoney valuation. This is common valuation trap number two.

Let's stay with our previous example of a $5 million investment at $20 million premoney. Assume that you have an existing option pool that has options representing 10 percent of the outstanding stock reserved and unissued. The VCs suggest that they want to see a 20 percent option pool. In this case, the extra 10 percent will come out of the premoney valuation, resulting in an effective premoney valuation of $18 million.

There is no magic number for the option pool, and this is often a key point of the pricing negotiation. The typical option pool ends up in a range of 10 percent to 20 percent, but if the investors believe that the option pool of the company should be increased, they will insist that the increase happens prior to the financing.

You have several negotiating approaches. You can fight the pool size, trying to get the VCs to end up at 15 percent instead of 20 percent. Or you can negotiate on the premoney valuation; accept a 20 percent pool but ask for a $22 million premoney valuation. Or you can suggest that the increase in the option pool gets added to the deal postmoney, which will result in the same premoney valuation but a higher postmoney one.

The Entrepreneur's Perspective

VCs will want to minimize their risk of future dilution as much as possible by making the option pool as large as possible up front. When you have this negotiation, you should come armed with an *option budget*. List out all of the hires you plan on making between today and your next anticipated financing date and the approximate option grant you think it will take to land each one of them. You should be prepared to have an option pool with more options than your budget calls for, but not necessarily by a huge margin. The option budget will be critical in this conversation with your potential investor.

Another economic term that you will encounter, especially in later stage financings, is *warrants* associated with financings. As with the stock option pool allocation, this is another way for an investor to sneak in a lower valuation for the company. A warrant is similar to a stock option; it is a right for an investor to purchase a certain number of shares at a predefined price for a certain number of years. For example, a 10-year warrant for 100,000 shares of Series A stock at $1 per share gives the warrant holder the option to buy 100,000 shares of Series A stock at $1 per share anytime in the next decade, regardless of what the stock is worth at the moment in time the investor avails himself of (or *exercises*) the warrant.

Warrants as part of a venture financing, especially in an early stage investment, tend to create a lot of unnecessary complexity and accounting headaches down the road. If the issue is simply one of price, we recommend the entrepreneur negotiate for a lower pre-money valuation to try to eliminate the warrants. Occasionally, this may be at cross-purposes with existing investors who, for some reason, want to artificially inflate the valuation, since the warrant value is rarely calculated as part of the valuation even though it impacts the future allocation of proceeds in a liquidity event.

There is one type of financing—the *bridge loan*—in which warrants are commonplace. A bridge loan occurs when an investor is planning to do a financing, but is waiting for additional investors to participate. In the bridge loan scenario the existing investor will make the investment as *convertible debt*, which will convert into equity at the price of the upcoming financing. Since the bridge loan investor took additional risk, he generally gets either a discount on the price of the equity (usually up to 20 percent) or warrants that effectively grant a discount (again usually up to 20 percent, although occasionally more). In bridge round cases, it's not worth fighting these warrants as long as they are structured reasonably.

The best way for you to negotiate a higher price is to have multiple VCs interested in investing in your company. This is Economics 101; if you have more demand (VCs interested) than supply (equity in your company to sell), then price will increase. In early rounds, your new investors will likely be looking for the lowest possible price that still leaves enough equity in the founders' and employees' hands. In later rounds, your existing investors will often argue for the highest price for new investors in order to limit the dilution of the existing investors. If there are no new investors interested in investing in your company, your existing investors will often argue for a price equal to (*flat round*) or lower than (*down round*) the price of the previous round. Finally, new investors will always argue for the lowest price they think will enable them to get a financing done, given the appetite (or lack thereof) of the existing investors for putting more money into the company. As an entrepreneur, you are faced with all of these contradictory motivations in a financing, reinforcing the truism that it is incredibly important to pick your early investors wisely, since they can materially help or hurt this process.

The Entrepreneur's Perspective

The best Plan A has a great Plan B standing behind it. The more potential investors you have interested in investing in your company, the better your negotiating position is. Spend as much time on your *best alternative to a negotiated agreement* (BATNA) as possible.

By now you may be wondering how VCs really value companies. It is not an exact science regardless of the number of spreadsheets involved. VCs typically take into account many factors when deciding how to value a potential investment—some are quantifiable whereas others are completely qualitative. Following are some of the different factors, along with brief explanations of what impacts them.

- *Stage of the company.* Early stage companies tend to have a valuation range that is determined more by the experience of the entrepreneurs, the amount of money being raised, and the perception of the overall opportunity. As companies mature, the historical financial performance and future financial projects start to have impact. In later stage companies, supply and demand for financing combined with financial performance dominate, as investors are beginning to look toward an imminent exit event.
- *Competition with other funding sources.* The simple time-tested rule for the entrepreneur is "more is better." When VCs feel like they are competing with other VCs for a deal, price

tends to increase. However, a word of caution—don't overplay competition that doesn't exist. If you do and get caught, you'll damage your current negotiating position, potentially lose the existing investor that you have at the table, and, if nothing else, lose all of your leverage in other aspects of the negotiation. Our belief is that you should always negotiate honestly. Over-representing your situation rarely ends well.

- *Experience of the entrepreneurs and leadership team.* The more experienced the entrepreneurs, the less risk, and, correspondingly, the higher the valuation.
- *The VC's natural entry point.* Some VCs are early stage investors and will invest only at low price points. For example, we know of one well-known early stage investor who publicly states the intention not to invest at a valuation above $10 million post-money. Later stage investors tend to be much less focused on a specific price level and are more focused on the specific status of the company. While VC firms often have stated strategies, it's often the case that they will diverge from these strategies, especially when markets heat up.
- *Numbers, numbers, numbers.* The numbers matter also. Whether it is past performance; predictions of the future; revenue; earnings before interest, taxes, depreciation, and amortization (EBITDA); cash burn; or head count, they each factor into the determination of price. That being said, don't believe everything your MBA professor told you about DCF (discounted cash flow, for those of you without an MBA), especially for early stage companies. Remember, the only thing you know for sure about your financial projections at the early stages is that they are wrong.
- *Current economic climate.* Though this is out of the control of the entrepreneur, it weighs heavily on pricing. When the macroeconomy is in the dumps, valuations are lower. When the macroeconomy is expanding, valuations go up. Specifically, valuations often expand quickly when there is future optimism forecasted about the macroeconomy. However, these events are not tightly correlated, especially in the technology sector.

Our best advice to entrepreneurs on maximizing price is to focus on what you can control and get several different VCs interested in your financing.

> ### The Entrepreneur's Perspective
>
> I encourage entrepreneurs not to take valuation personally. Just because VCs say their take is that your business is worth $6 million, when your take is that your business is worth $10 million, doesn't mean that they lack appreciation for you as a CEO or your business's future potential. It means they are negotiating a deal to their advantage, just as you would.

Liquidation Preference

The liquidation preference is the next most important economic term after price and impacts how the proceeds are shared in a liquidity event, which is usually defined as a sale of the company or the majority of the company's assets. The liquidation preference is especially important in cases in which a company is sold for less than the amount of capital invested.

There are two components that make up what most people call the liquidation preference: the actual preference and participation. To be accurate, the term *liquidation preference* should pertain only to money returned to a particular series of the company's stock ahead of other series of stock. Consider, for instance, the following language:

> Liquidation Preference: In the event of any liquidation or winding up of the Company, the holders of the Series A Preferred shall be entitled to receive in preference to the holders of the Common Stock a per share amount equal to [X] times the Original Purchase Price plus any declared but unpaid dividends (the Liquidation Preference).

This is the actual preference. In this language, a certain multiple of the original investment per share is returned to the investor before the common stock receives any consideration. For many years, a 1× liquidation preference, or simply the amount of money invested, was the standard. In 2001, as the Internet bubble burst, investors often increased this multiple, sometimes as high as 10× (10 times the amount of money invested). Over time, rational thought prevailed and this number has generally returned to 1×.

The next thing to consider is whether the investors' shares are participating. While many people consider the term *liquidation preference* to refer to both the preference and the participation, it's important to separate the concepts. There are three varieties of participation: full participation, capped participation, and no participation.

Fully participating stock will receive its participation amount and then share in the liquidation proceeds on an *as-converted basis* where "as-converted" means as if the stock were converted into common stock based on its conversion ratio. The provision normally looks like this:

> Participation: After the payment of the Liquidation Preference to the holders of the Series A Preferred, the remaining assets shall be distributed ratably to the holders of the Common Stock and the Series A Preferred on a common equivalent basis.

Capped participation indicates that the stock will share in the liquidation proceeds on an as-converted basis until a certain multiple return is reached. Sample language is as follows.

> Participation: After the payment of the Liquidation Preference to the holders of the Series A Preferred, the remaining assets shall be distributed ratably to the holders of the Common Stock and the Series A Preferred on a common equivalent basis, provided that the holders of Series A Preferred will stop participating once they have received a total liquidation amount per share equal to [X] times the Original Purchase Price, plus any declared but unpaid dividends. Thereafter, the remaining assets shall be distributed ratably to the holders of the Common Stock.

One interesting thing to note in this section is the actual meaning of the multiple of the original purchase price (the [X]). If the participation multiple is 3 (three times the original purchase price), it would mean that the preferred would stop participation (on a per-share basis) once 300 percent of its original purchase price was returned, including any amounts paid out on the liquidation preference. This is not an additional 3× return, but rather an additional 2×, assuming the liquidation preference was a 1× money-back return. Perhaps this correlation with the actual preference is the reason the term *liquidation preference* has come to include both the preference and participation terms. If the series is not participating, it will not have a paragraph that looks like the preceding ones.

No participation indicates that the stock doesn't participate. In this case, the investor either gets the liquidation preference or the stock converts into common shares and the investor gets their as-converted basis.

Since we've been talking about liquidation preferences, it's important to define what a *liquidation event* is. Often, entrepreneurs think of a liquidation event as a bad thing, such as a bankruptcy or a winding down. In VC-speak, a liquidation is actually tied to a *liquidity event* in which the shareholders receive proceeds for their equity in a company, and it includes mergers, *acquisitions*, or a change of control of the company. As a result, the liquidation preference section determines the allocation of proceeds in both good times and bad. Standard language defining a liquidation event looks like this:

> A merger, acquisition, sale of voting control, or sale of substantially all of the assets of the Company in which the shareholders of the Company do not own a majority of the outstanding shares of the surviving corporation shall be deemed to be a liquidation.

Ironically, lawyers don't necessarily agree on a standard definition of a liquidation event. Jason once had an entertaining and unpleasant debate during a guest lecture he gave at his alma mater law school with a partner from a major Chicago law firm. At the time, this partner was teaching a venture class that semester and claimed that an IPO should be considered a liquidation event. His theory was that an IPO was the same as a merger, that the company was going away, and thus the investors should get their proceeds. Even if such a theory would be accepted by an investment banker who would be willing to take the company public (there's not a chance, in our opinion), it makes no sense, as an IPO is simply another funding event for the company, not a liquidation of the company. In fact, in almost all IPO scenarios, the VCs preferred stock is converted to common stock as part of the IPO, eliminating the issue around a liquidity event in the first place.

Let's explore several different cases. To keep it simple, let's assume that there has been only one round of financing (a Series A investment) of $5 million at a $10 million premoney valuation. In this case, the Series A investors own 33.3 percent of the company [$5m/($10m + $5m)] and the entrepreneurs own 66.7 percent of the company. To make the math a little easier, we'll round it to 33 percent/67 percent.

Now, assume that the company has an offer to be acquired for $30 million.

Case 1: 1× preference, nonparticipating: In this case, the Series A investors will get 33 percent, or $10 million, and the entrepreneurs will get 67 percent, or $20 million.

Case 2: 1× preference, participating: In this case, the Series A investors will get the first $5 million and then 33 percent of the remaining amount, or $8.3 million (33 percent of $25 million) for a total return of $13.3 million. The entrepreneurs will get 67 percent of the $25 million, or $16.7 million.

Case 3: 1× preference, participating with a 3× cap: In this case, the preferred will not reach the cap ($15 million), so this will be the same as Case 2.

Now, assume the purchase price is $100 million and there has still been only one Series A financing of $5 million at a $15 million postmoney valuation.

Case 1: 1× preference, nonparticipating: The Series A investors will get 33 percent, or $33 million, and the entrepreneurs will get 67 percent, or $67 million.

Case 2: 1× preference, participating: Again, the Series A investors get the first $5 million and then 33 percent of the remaining $95 million, or $31.35, for a total of $36.35. The entrepreneurs get 67 percent of the remaining $95 million, or $63.65 million.

Case 3: 1× preference, participating with a 3× cap: In this example, the Series A makes a return better than 3×, so the participation doesn't happen and the results are the same as in Case 1.

As you can see from this example, the participation feature has a lot of impact at relatively low outcomes and less impact (on a percentage of the deal basis) at higher outcomes. The participation feature will also matter a lot more as more money is raised that has the participation feature (e.g., Series B and C). To understand this, let's do one last example, this time of a company that has raised $50 million where the investors own 60 percent and the entrepreneurs own 40 percent. Assume the company is being acquired for $100 million.

Case 1: 1× preference, nonparticipating: Investors get 60 percent, or $60 million, and the entrepreneurs get 40 percent, or $40 million.

Case 2: 1× preference, participating: Investors get the first $50 million, and then 60 percent of the remaining $50 million ($30 million) for a total of $80 million. The entrepreneurs get 40 percent of the remaining $50 million, or $20 million.

Case 3: 1× preference, participating with a 3× cap: Since the investors won't make greater than 3× on this deal, this is the same as Case 2.

Liquidation preferences are usually easy to understand and assess when dealing with a Series A term sheet. It gets much more complicated to understand what is going on as a company matures and sells additional series of equity, since understanding how liquidation preferences work between the various series is often mathematically, and structurally, challenging. As with many VC-related issues, the approach to liquidation preferences among multiple series of stock varies and is often overly complex for no apparent reason.

There are two primary approaches:

1. The follow-on investors will stack their preferences on top of each other (known as *stacked preferences*) where Series B gets its preference first, then Series A.
2. The series are equivalent in status (known as *pari passu* or *blended preferences*) so that Series A and B share proratably until the preferences are returned.

Determining which approach to use is a black art that is influenced by the relative negotiating power of the investors involved, ability of the company to go elsewhere for additional financing, economic dynamics of the existing capital structure, and the current phase of the moon.

Let's look at an example. This time, our example company has raised two rounds of financing, a Series A ($5 million invested at a $10 million premoney valuation) and a Series B ($20 million invested at a $30 million premoney valuation). Now, let's deal with a low outcome, one where the liquidation preference is going to come into play, namely a sale of the company for $15 million.

If the preference is stacked, the Series B investors will get the entire $15 million. In fact, in this case it won't matter what the pre-money valuation of the Series B was; they'll get 100 percent of the consideration regardless.

However, if the preference is blended, the Series A will get 20 percent of every dollar returned (in this case $3 million) and the Series B will get 80 percent of every dollar returned (or $12 million), based on their relative amounts of the capital invested in the company.

In each of these cases the entrepreneurs will receive nothing regardless of whether the preference is participating or nonparticipating since the preference is $25 million and the company is being sold for $15 million, or less than the preference.

Note that investors get either the liquidation preference and participation amounts (if any) or what they would get on a fully converted common holding, at their election; they do not get both. Realize, however, that in the fully participating case the investors get their participation amount and then receive what they would get on a fully converted common holding basis.

In early stage financings, it's actually in the best interest of both the investor and the entrepreneur to have a simple liquidation preference and no participation. In future rounds, the terms are often at the minimum equivalent to the early stage terms. So, if you have a participating preferred in a seed round, you could expect to have a participating preferred in all subsequent rounds. In this case, if the seed investor doesn't participate in future rounds, his economics in many outcomes could actually be worse with the participation feature. As a result, we recommend to entrepreneurs and our VC co-investors to keep it simple and lightweight in early rounds.

Most professional investors will not want to gouge a company with excessive liquidation preferences since the greater the liquidation preference, the lower the potential value of the management or employee equity. There's a fine balance here and each case is situation specific, but a rational investor will want a combination of the best price while ensuring maximum motivation of management and employees. Obviously, what happens in the end is a negotiation and depends on the stage of the company, bargaining strength, and existing capital structure; but in general most companies and their investors will reach a reasonable compromise regarding these provisions.

The Entrepreneur's Perspective

Liquidation preference is a critical term that is part of most equity financings other than small angel financings. Participating preferred deals have become an unfortunate standard over the years where VCs have essentially decided on a new standard floor for deals that require the repayment of principal as well as a common stock interest in the company on the sale of a company. In the mid-1990s, companies used to negotiate so-called kickouts whereby participation rights went away as long as the company had achieved a meaningful return for the VC (2× to 3×). Entrepreneurs should band together to reinstate this as a standard!

Anything other than a straight participating preferred security, such as multiple preferences, is just greedy on the part of VCs and should be a red flag to you about the investor.

Pay-to-Play

The *pay-to-play* provision is another important economic term that is usually relevant in a down round financing and can be very useful to the entrepreneur in situations where the company is struggling and needs another financing. A typical pay-to-play provision follows:

> Pay-to-Play: In the event of a Qualified Financing (as defined below), shares of Series A Preferred held by any Investor which is offered the right to participate but does not participate fully in such financing by purchasing at least its pro rata portion as calculated above under "Right of First Refusal" below will be converted into Common Stock.
>
> A Qualified Financing is the next round of financing after the Series A financing by the Company that is approved by the Board of Directors who determine in good faith that such portion must be purchased pro rata among the stockholders of the Company subject to this provision. Such determination will be made regardless of whether the price is higher or lower than any series of Preferred Stock.

At the turn of the millennium, a pay-to-play provision was rarely seen. After the Internet bubble burst in 2001, it became ubiquitous.

Interestingly, this is a term that most companies and their investors can agree on if they approach it from the right perspective.

In a pay-to-play provision, investors must keep participating proratably in future financings (paying) in order to not have their preferred stock converted to common stock (playing) in the company.

There are various levels of intensity of the pay-to-play provision. The preceding one is pretty aggressive when compared to this softer one:

> If any holder of Series A Preferred Stock fails to participate in the next Qualified Financing (as defined below), on a pro rata basis (according to its total equity ownership immediately before such financing) of their Series A Preferred investment, then such holder will have the Series A Preferred Stock it owns converted into Common Stock of the Company. If such holder participates in the next Qualified Financing but not to the full extent of its pro rata share, then only a percentage of its Series A Preferred Stock will be converted into Common Stock (under the same terms as in the preceding sentence), with such percentage being equal to the percent of its pro rata contribution that it failed to contribute.
>
> When determining the number of shares held by an Investor or whether this "Pay-to-Play" provision has been satisfied, all shares held by or purchased in the Qualified Financing by affiliated investment funds shall be aggregated. An Investor shall be entitled to assign its rights to participate in this financing and future financings to its affiliated funds and to investors in the Investor and/or its affiliated funds, including funds that are not current stockholders of the Company.

We believe that pay-to-play provisions are generally good for the company and its investors. It causes the investors to stand up at the time of their original investment and agree to support the company during its life cycle. If they do not, the stock they have is converted from preferred to common and they lose the rights associated with the preferred stock. When our co-investors push back on this term, we ask: "Why? Are you not going to fund the company in the future if other investors agree to?" Remember, this is not a lifetime guarantee of investment; rather, if other prior investors decide to invest in future rounds in the company, there will be a strong incentive for all of the prior investors to invest or subject themselves to total or partial conversion of their holdings to common stock. A pay-to-play term ensures that all the investors agree in advance to the rules of engagement concerning future financings.

The pay-to-play provision impacts the economics of the deal by reducing liquidation preferences for the nonparticipating investors. It also impacts the control of the deal since it reshuffles the future preferred shareholder base by ensuring that only the committed investors continue to have preferred stock and the corresponding rights that go along with preferred stock.

When companies are doing well, the pay-to-play provision is often waived since a new investor wants to take a large part of the new round. This is a good problem for a company to have, as it typically means there is an up-round financing, existing investors can help drive company-friendly terms in the new round, and the investor syndicate increases in strength by virtue of new capital (and, presumably, another helpful co-investor) in the deal.

The Entrepreneur's Perspective

This pay-to-play provision is pretty good for you as an entrepreneur, at least as it's described here. Conversion to common is no big deal in the grand scheme of things. What you want to avoid is a pay-to-play scenario where your VC has the right to force a recapitalization of the company (e.g., a financing at a $0 premoney valuation, or something suitably low) if fellow investors don't play into a new round.

A provision like this can be particularly bad for less sophisticated angel investors (e.g., your friends and family) if they don't have the understanding or resources to back up their initial investment with future follow-on investments, and can make for uncomfortable conversations around family events.

There are many circumstances where reasonable investors who like the company can't or won't participate in a financing—their venture fund is over, or they are strategic or angel investors and don't have the funds or charter to continue investing—and you and they shouldn't be punished excessively for not participating (remember, a recapitalization hurts you, too, even if you get new options, which always carry vesting, to "top you off"). But conversion to common for lack of follow-on investment is appropriate.

Vesting

Although vesting is a simple concept, it can have profound and unexpected implications. Typically, stock and options will vest over four years. This means that you have to be around for four years to own all of your stock or options (from this point forward, we'll simply refer to the equity that the entrepreneurs and employees receive as stock, although exactly the same logic applies to options). If you leave the company before the end of the four-year period, the vesting formula applies and you get only a percentage of your stock. As a result, many entrepreneurs view vesting as a way for VCs to control them, their involvement, and their ownership in a company, which, while it can be true, is only a part of the story.

A typical stock-vesting clause looks as follows:

> Stock Vesting: All stock and stock equivalents issued after the Closing to employees, directors, consultants, and other service providers will be subject to vesting provisions below unless different vesting is approved by the majority (including at least one director designated by the Investors) consent of the Board of Directors (the "Required Approval"): 25 percent to vest at the end of the first year following such issuance, with the remaining 75 percent to vest monthly over the next three years. The repurchase option shall provide that upon termination of the employment of the shareholder, with or without cause, the Company or its assignee (to the extent permissible under applicable securities law qualification) retains the option to repurchase at the lower of cost or the current fair market value any unvested shares held by such shareholder. Any issuance of shares in excess of the Employee Pool not approved by the Required Approval will be a dilutive event requiring adjustment of the conversion price as provided above and will be subject to the Investors' first offer rights.
>
> The outstanding Common Stock currently held by _____ and _____ (the "Founders") will be subject to similar vesting terms provided that the Founders shall be credited with [one year] of vesting as of the Closing, with their remaining unvested shares to vest monthly over three years.

Industry standard vesting for early stage companies is a one-year cliff and monthly vesting thereafter for a total of four years. This means that if you leave before the first year is up, you haven't vested any of your stock. After a year, you have vested 25 percent (that's the "cliff"). Then you begin vesting monthly (or quarterly, or annually) over the remaining period. If you have a monthly vest with a one-year cliff and you leave the company after 18 months, you'll have vested 37.5 percent (or 18/48) of your stock.

Often, founders will get somewhat different vesting provisions than the rest of the employees. A common term is the second paragraph of the example clause, where the founders receive one year of vesting credit at the closing of the financing and then vest the balance of their stock over the remaining 36 months. This type of vesting arrangement is typical in cases where the founders have started the company a year or more earlier than the VC investment and want to get some credit for existing time served. In cases where the founders started the company within a year of the first VC investment, they will occasionally be able to argue for vesting back to the inception of the company.

Unvested stock typically disappears into the ether when someone leaves the company. The equity doesn't get reallocated; rather, it gets reabsorbed and everyone (VCs, stockholders, and option holders) all benefit ratably from the increase in ownership, also known as *reverse dilution*. In the case of founders' stock, the unvested stuff just vanishes. In the case of unvested employee options, it usually goes back into the option pool to be reissued to future employees.

In some cases, founders own their stock outright through a purchase at the time that the company is established. While the description of what happens to this founders' stock is often referred to as vesting, it's actually a buy-back right of the company. Though there are technically the same outcomes, the legal language around this is somewhat different and matters for tax purposes.

The Entrepreneur's Perspective

How a founder's stock vests is important. Although simple vesting can work, you should consider alternative strategies such as allowing you to purchase your unvested stock at the same price as the financing if you leave the company, protecting your position for a termination "without cause," or treating your vesting as a *clawback* with an Internal Revenue Code Section 83(b) election so you can lock in long-term capital gains tax rates early on (which is discussed later in this book).

A key component of vesting is defining what, if anything, happens to vesting schedules upon a merger. *Single-trigger acceleration* refers to automatic accelerated vesting upon a merger. *Double-trigger acceleration* refers to two events needing to take place before accelerated vesting, specifically an acquisition of the company combined with the employee in question being fired by the acquiring company.

In VC-funded deals, a double trigger is much more common than a single trigger. Acceleration on change of control is often a contentious point of negotiation between founders and VCs, as the founders will want to get all their stock in a transaction—"Hey, we earned it!"—and VCs will want to minimize the impact of the outstanding equity on their share of the purchase price. Most acquirers will want there to be some forward-looking incentive for founders, management, and employees, so they usually prefer some unvested equity to exist to help motivate folks to stick around for a period of time postacquisition. In the absence of this, the acquirer will include a separate management retention incentive as part of the deal value. Since this management retention piece is included in the value of the transaction, it effectively reduces the consideration that gets allocated to the equity owners of the company, including the VCs and any founders who are no longer actively involved in the company. This often frustrates VCs since it puts them at cross-purposes with management in an acquisition negotiation—everyone should be negotiating to maximize the value for all shareholders, not just specifically for themselves. Although the actual legal language is not very interesting, it is included here:

> In the event of a merger, consolidation, sale of assets, or other change of control of the Company and should an Employee be terminated without cause within one year after such event, such person shall be entitled to [one year] of additional vesting. Other than the foregoing, there shall be no accelerated vesting in any event.

Structuring acceleration on change-of-control terms used to be a huge deal in the 1990s when pooling of interests was an accepted form of accounting treatment, since there were significant constraints on any modifications to vesting agreements. Pooling was abolished in early 2000 and, under current acquisition accounting treatment (also known as purchase accounting) there is no meaningful accounting impact in a merger of changing the vesting arrangements (including accelerating vesting). As a result, we usually recommend a balanced approach to acceleration such as a double trigger with one-year acceleration and recognize that this will often be negotiated during an acquisition. It's important to recognize that many VCs have a distinct point of view on this; some VCs will never do a deal with single-trigger acceleration, whereas some VCs don't really care very much. As in any negotiation, make sure you are not negotiating against a point of principle, as VCs will often say, "That's how it is and we won't do anything different."

Recognize that vesting works for the founders as well as the VCs. We have been involved in a number of situations where one founder didn't stay with the company very long either by choice or because the other founders wanted him to leave the company. In these situations, if there hadn't been vesting provisions, the person who didn't stay at the company would have walked away with all of his stock and the remaining founders would have had no differential ownership going forward. By vesting each founder, there is a clear incentive to work your hardest and participate constructively in the team, beyond the elusive founder's moral imperative. The same rule applies to employees; since equity is another form of compensation, vesting is the mechanism to ensure the equity is earned over time.

Time to exit has a huge impact on the relevancy of vesting. In the late 1990s, when companies often reached an exit event within two years of being founded, the vesting provisions, especially acceleration clauses, mattered a huge amount to the founders. In a market where the typical gestation period of an early stage company is five to seven years, most people, especially founders and early employees who stay with a company, will be fully (or mostly) vested at the time of an exit event.

While it's easy to set vesting up as a contentious issue between founders and VCs, we recommend the founding entrepreneurs view vesting as an overall alignment tool—for themselves, their cofounders, early employees, and future employees. Anyone who has experienced an unfair vesting situation will have strong feelings about it; a balanced approach and consistency are key to making vesting provisions work long-term in a company.

The Entrepreneur's Perspective

While single-trigger acceleration might seem appealing, double-trigger acceleration with some boundaries makes a lot of sense. Any entrepreneur who has been on the buy side of an acquisition will tell you that having one or two years' worth of guaranteed transition on the part of an acquired management team is critical to an acquisition's financial success.

Employee Pool

Another economic term that matters, but is often not focused on until the end of the negotiation, is the *employee pool* (also known as the *option pool*). The employee pool is the amount of the company that is reserved for future issuance to employees. Typical language follows:

> Employee Pool: Prior to the Closing, the Company will reserve shares of its Common Stock so that __ percent of its fully diluted capital stock following the issuance of its Series A Preferred is available for future issuances to directors, officers, employees, and consultants. The term "Employee Pool" shall include both shares reserved for issuance as stated above, as well as current options outstanding, which aggregate amount is approximately __ percent of the Company's fully diluted capital stock following the issuance of its Series A Preferred.

The employee pool is called out as a separate section in order to clarify the capital structure and specifically define the percentage of the company that will be allocated to the option pool associated with the financing. Since a *capitalization table* is almost always included with the term sheet, this section is redundant, but exists so there is no confusion about the size of the option pool.

It is important to understand the impact of the size of the pool on the valuation of the financing. As with premoney and postmoney valuations, VCs often sneak in additional economics for themselves by increasing the amount of the option pool on a premoney basis.

Let's go through an example. Assume that a $2 million financing is being done at a $10 million postmoney valuation. In this case, the new investors get 20 percent of the company for $2 million and the effective postmoney valuation is $10 million. Before the financing there is a 10 percent unallocated option pool. However, in the term sheet, the investors put a provision that the postfinancing unallocated option pool will be 20 percent. This results in a postfinancing ownership split of 20 percent to the new investors, 60 percent to the old shareholders, and an unallocated employee pool of 20 percent.

In contrast, if the 10 percent option pool that previously existed was simply rolled over, the postmoney allocation would still be 20 percent to new investors, but the old shareholders would get 70 percent and the unallocated option pool would be 10 percent.

While in both cases the investors end up with 20 percent, the old investors have 10 percent less ownership in the case of the 20 percent option pool. Although the additional ownership will ultimately end up in the hands of future employees, it is effectively coming out of the old shareholders rather than being shared between the new investors and the old shareholders. This will result in a lower price per share for the new investors and effectively a lower premoney valuation.

If the VC is pushing for a larger option pool to come out of the premoney valuation but the entrepreneur feels that there is enough in the pool to meet the company's needs over the time frame of this financing, the entrepreneur can say, "Look, I strongly believe we have enough options to cover our needs. Let's go with it at my proposed level and if we should need to expand the option pool before the next financing, we will provide full antidilution protection for you to cover that."

Antidilution

The final key economic provision is *antidilution*. A typical antidilution clause in a term sheet follows:

> Antidilution Provisions: The conversion price of the Series A Preferred will be subject to a [full ratchet/broad-based/narrow-based weighted average] adjustment to reduce dilution in the event that the Company issues additional equity securities—other than shares (i) reserved as employee shares described under the Company's option pool; (ii) shares issued for consideration other than cash pursuant to a merger, consolidation, acquisition, or similar business combination approved by the Board; (iii) shares issued pursuant to any equipment loan or

leasing arrangement, real property leasing arrangement, or debt financing from a bank or similar financial institution approved by the Board; and (iv) shares with respect to which the holders of a majority of the outstanding Series A Preferred waive their antidilution rights—at a purchase price less than the applicable conversion price. In the event of an issuance of stock involving tranches or other multiple closings, the antidilution adjustment shall be calculated as if all stock was issued at the first closing. The conversion price will also be subject to proportional adjustment for stock splits, stock dividends, combinations, recapitalizations, and the like.

Yeah, we agree—that's a mouthful. It's also a clause that often trips up entrepreneurs. While the antidilution provision is used to protect investors in the event a company issues equity at a lower valuation than in previous financing rounds, it is also an excuse for lawyers to use a spreadsheet. There are two varieties: *weighted average antidilution* and *ratchet-based antidilution.*

Full ratchet antidilution means that if the company issues shares at a price lower than the price for the series with the full ratchet provision, then the earlier round price is effectively reduced to the price of the new issuance. One can get creative and do partial ratchets, such as half ratchets or two-thirds ratchets, which are less harsh but rarely seen.

Full ratchets came into vogue in the 2001–2003 time frame when down rounds were all the rage, but the most common antidilution provision is based on the weighted average concept, which takes into account the magnitude of the lower-priced issuance, not just the actual valuation. In a full ratchet world, if the company sold one share of its stock to someone for a price lower than the previous round, all of the previous round stock would be repriced to the new issuance price. In a weighted average world, the number of shares issued at the reduced price is considered in the repricing of the previous round. Mathematically (and this is where the lawyers get to show off their math skills—although you'll notice there are no exponents or summation signs anywhere) it works as follows:

$$NCP = OCP * \frac{CSO + CSP}{CSO + CSAP}$$

where:

NCP = new conversion price

OCP = old conversion price

CSO = common stock outstanding

CSP = common stock purchasable with consideration received by company (i.e., what the buyer should have bought if it hadn't been a down round issuance)

CSAP = common stock actually purchased in subsequent issuance (i.e., what the buyer actually bought)

Note that despite the fact one is buying preferred stock, the calculations are always done on an as-if-converted (to common stock) basis. The company is not issuing more shares; rather, it determines a new conversion price for the previous series of stock. Alternatively, the company can issue more shares, but we think this is a silly and unnecessarily complicated approach that merely increases the amount the lawyers can bill the company for the financing. Consequently, antidilution provisions usually generate a *conversion price adjustment*.

You might note the term *broad-based* in describing weighted average antidilution. What makes the provision broad-based versus narrow-based is the definition of common stock outstanding (CSO). A broad-based weighted average provision encompasses both the company's common stock outstanding (including all common stock issuable upon conversion of its preferred stock) as well as the number of shares of common stock that could be obtained by converting all other options, rights, and securities (including employee options). A narrow-based provision will not include these other convertible securities and will limit the calculation to only currently outstanding securities. The number of shares and how you count them matter; make sure you are agreeing on the same definition, as you'll often find different lawyers arguing over what to include or not include in the definitions.

In our example language, we've included a section that is generally referred to as "antidilution *carve-outs*"—the section "other than shares (i) ... (iv)." These are the standard exceptions for shares granted at lower prices for which antidilution does not apply. From a company and entrepreneur perspective, more exceptions are better, and most investors will accept these carve-outs without much argument.

One particular item to note is the last carve-out:

(iv) shares with respect to which the holders of a majority of the outstanding Series A Preferred waive their antidilution rights.

This is a carve-out that started appearing recently, which we have found to be very helpful in deals where a majority of the Series A investors agree to further fund a company in a follow-on financing, but the price will be lower than the original Series A. In this example, several minority investors signaled they were not planning to invest in the new round, as they would have preferred to sit back and increase their ownership stake via the antidilution provision. Having the larger investors (the majority of the class) step up and vote to carve the financing out of the antidilution terms was a bonus for the company common stockholders and employees, who would have suffered the dilution of additional antidilution from investors who were not continuing to participate in financing the company. This approach encourages the minority investors to participate in the round in order to protect themselves from dilution.

Occasionally, antidilution will be absent in a Series A term sheet. Investors love precedent (e.g., the new investor says, "I want what the last guy got, plus more"). In many cases antidilution provisions hurt Series A investors more than later investors if you assume the Series A price is the low-water mark for the company. For instance, if the Series A price is $1.00, the Series B price is $5.00, and the Series C price is $3.00, then the Series B benefits from the antidilution provision at the expense of the Series A. Our experience is that antidilution is usually requested despite this, as Series B investors will most likely always ask for it and, since they do, the Series A investors proactively ask for it anyway.

In addition to economic impacts, antidilution provisions can have control impacts. First, the existence of an antidilution provision will motivate the company to issue new rounds of stock at higher valuations because of the impact of antidilution protection on the common stockholders. In some cases, a company may pass on taking an additional investment at a lower valuation, although practically speaking, this happens only when a company has other alternatives to the financing. A recent phenomenon is to tie antidilution calculations to milestones the investors have set for the company, resulting in a conversion price adjustment in the case that the company does not meet certain revenue, product development, or other business milestones. In this situation, the antidilution adjustment occurs automatically if the company does not meet its objectives, unless the investor waives it after the fact. This creates a powerful incentive for the company to accomplish its investor-determined goals. We tend to avoid this approach, as blindly hitting predetermined product and sales milestones set at the time of a financing is not always best for the long-term development of a company, especially if these goals end up creating a diverging set of objectives between management and the investors as the business evolves.

Antidilution provisions are almost always part of a financing, so understanding the nuances and knowing which aspects to negotiate are an important part of the entrepreneur's tool kit. We advise you not to get hung up in trying to eliminate antidilution provisions. Instead, focus on minimizing their impact and building value in your company after the financing so they don't ever come into play.

CHAPTER 5

Control Terms of the Term Sheet

The terms we discussed in the preceding chapter define the economics of a deal; the next batch of terms define the control parameters of a deal. VCs care about control provisions in order to keep an eye on their investment as well as comply with certain federal tax statutes that are a result of the types of investors that invest in VC funds. While VCs often have less than 50 percent ownership of a company, they usually have a variety of control terms that effectively give them control of many activities of the company.

In this chapter we discuss the following terms: board of directors, protective provisions, drag-along rights, and conversion.

Board of Directors

One of the key control mechanisms is the process for electing the board of directors. The entrepreneur should think carefully about what the proper balance should be among investor, company, founder, and outside representation on the board.

The Entrepreneur's Perspective

Electing a board of directors is an important, and delicate, point. Your board is your inner sanctum, your strategic planning department, and your judge, jury, and executioner all at once. Some VCs are terrible board members, even if they're good investors and nice people.

A typical board of directors clause follows:

> Board of Directors: The size of the Company's Board of Directors shall be set at [X]. The Board shall initially be comprised of _____, as the Investor representative[s] _____, _____, and _____. At each meeting for the election of directors, the holders of the Series A Preferred, voting as a separate class, shall be entitled to elect [X] member[s] of the Company's Board of Directors which director shall be designated by Investor, the holders of Common Stock, voting as a separate class, shall be entitled to elect [X] member[s], and the remaining directors will be [Option 1: mutually agreed upon by the Common and Preferred, voting together as a single class] [or Option 2: chosen by the mutual consent of the Board of Directors].

If a subset of the board is being chosen by more than one constituency (e.g., two directors chosen by the investors, two by founders or common stockholders, and one by mutual consent), you should consider what is best: chosen by mutual consent of the board (one person, one vote) or voted upon on the basis of proportional share ownership on a common-as-converted basis.

VCs will often want to include a board observer as part of the agreement either instead of or in addition to an official member of the board. This is typical and usually helpful, as many VC partners have an associate who works with them on their companies.

The Entrepreneur's Perspective

Be wary of observers. Sometimes they add no value yet they do take up seats at the table. Often, it's not about who votes at a board meeting, but the discussion that occurs, so observers can sway the balance of a board. You don't want to find yourself with a pre-revenue company and 15 people around the table at a board meeting.

Many investors will mandate that one of the board members chosen by common stockholders be the then-serving CEO of the company. This can be tricky if the CEO is the same as one of the key founders (often you'll see language giving the right to a board seat to one of the founders and a separate board seat to the then CEO), consuming two of the common board seats. Then, if the CEO changes, so does that board seat.

Let's go through two examples: an early stage board for a company that has raised its first round of capital and the board of a company that is mature and contemplating an initial public offering (IPO).

In the case of the early stage board, there will typically be five board members:

1. Founder
2. CEO
3. VC
4. A second VC
5. An outside board member

This would be the default case for a balanced board that gives the VC enough influence to be comfortable without having control over the board. Correspondingly, the founder and CEO will have the same number of seats as the VCs, and the outside board member will be able to help resolve any conflicts that arise as well as be a legitimately nonconflicted board member.

In the case of a mature board, you'll typically see more board members (seven to nine) with more outside board members. The CEO and one of the founders are on this board along with a few of the VCs (depending on the amount of money raised). However, the majority of the additions to the board are outside board members, typically experienced entrepreneurs or executives in the domain in which the company is operating.

While it is appropriate for board members and observers to be reimbursed for their reasonable out-of-pocket costs for attending board meetings, we rarely see board members receive cash compensation for serving on the board of a private company. Outside board members are usually compensated with stock options—just like key employees—and are often invited to invest money in the company alongside the VCs.

Protective Provisions

The next key control term you will encounter in the term sheet is the *protective provisions*. Protective provisions are effectively veto rights that investors have on certain actions by the company. Not surprisingly, these provisions protect VCs, although unfortunately not from themselves.

The protective provisions are often hotly negotiated but over time have mostly become standardized. Entrepreneurs would like to see few or no protective provisions in their documents. In contrast, VCs would like to have some veto-level control over a set of actions the company could take, especially when it impacts the VCs' economic position.

A typical protective provision clause looks as follows:

> Protective Provisions: For so long as any shares of Series A Preferred remain outstanding, consent of the holders of at least a majority of the Series A Preferred shall be required for any action, whether directly or through any merger, recapitalization, or similar event, that (i) alters or changes the rights, preferences, or privileges of the Series A Preferred; (ii) increases or decreases the authorized number of shares of Common or Preferred Stock; (iii) creates (by reclassification or otherwise) any new class or series of shares having rights, preferences, or privileges senior to or on a parity with the Series A Preferred; (iv) results in the redemption or repurchase of any shares of Common Stock (other than pursuant to equity incentive agreements with service providers giving the Company the right to repurchase shares upon the termination of services); (v) results in any merger, other corporate reorganization, sale of control, or any transaction in which all or substantially all of the assets of the Company are sold; (vi) amends or waives any provision of the Company's Certificate of Incorporation or Bylaws; (vii) increases or decreases the authorized size of the Company's Board of Directors; (viii) results in the payment or declaration of any dividend on any shares of Common or Preferred Stock; or (ix) results in issuance of debt in excess of $100,000.

Let's translate this into what the VC is trying to protect against. Simply, unless the VC agrees, don't:

- Change the terms of stock owned by the VC.
- Authorize the creation of more stock.
- Issue stock senior or equal to the VC's.
- Buy back any common stock.

- Sell the company.
- Change the certificate of incorporation or bylaws.
- Change the size of board of directors.
- Pay or declare a dividend.
- Borrow money.

Subsection (ix) of the protective provision clause is often the first thing that gets changed by raising the debt threshold to something higher, as long as the company is a real operating business rather than an early stage startup. Another easily accepted change is to add a minimum threshold of preferred shares outstanding for the protective provisions to apply, keeping the protective provisions from lingering on forever when the capital structure is changed—through either a positive or a negative event.

Many company counsels will ask for *materiality qualifiers*—for instance, that the word *material* or *materially* be inserted in front of subsections (i), (ii), and (vi) in the example. We always decline this request, not to be stubborn, but because we don't really know what *material* means (if you ask a judge or read any case law, that will not help you, either), and we believe that specificity is more important than debating reasonableness. Remember that these are protective provisions; they don't eliminate the ability to do these things, but simply require consent of the investors. As long as things are not material from the VC's point of view, the consent to do these things will be granted. We'd always rather be clear up front what the rules of engagement are rather than have a debate over what the word *material* means in the middle of a situation where these protective provisions might come into play.

The Entrepreneur's Perspective

As far as the example protective provision clause is concerned, (i) fair is fair; (ii) fair is fair; (iii) fair is fair; (iv) this should be positive for VCs, but not a big deal; (v) this is critical as long as Series A preferred holders represent, in aggregate, enough of your capitalization table to be relevant; (vi) makes sense; (vii) this is critical as long as Series A preferred holders represent, in aggregate, enough of your cap table to be relevant; (viii) you will never have to worry about this; (ix) this is fine, though you should try to get a higher limit or an exclusion for equipment financing in the normal course of business.

When future financing rounds occur (e.g., Series B, a new class of preferred stock), there is always a discussion as to how the protective provisions will work with regard to the new class. There are two cases: the Series B gets its own protective provisions or the Series B investors vote alongside the original investors as a single class. Entrepreneurs almost always will want a single vote for all the investors, as the separate investor class protective provision vote means the company now has two classes of potential veto constituents to deal with. Normally, new investors will ask for a separate vote, as their interests may diverge from those of the original investors due to different pricing, different risk profiles, and a false need for overall control. However, many experienced investors will align with the entrepreneur's point of view of not wanting separate class votes, as they do not want the potential headaches of another equity class vetoing an important company action. If Series B investors are the same as Series A investors, this is an irrelevant discussion and it should be easy for everyone to default to voting as a single class. If you have new investors in the Series B, be wary of inappropriate veto rights for small investors; for example, the consent percentage required is 90 percent instead of a majority (50.1 percent), enabling a new investor who owns only 10.1 percent of the financing to effectively assert control over the protective provisions through his vote.

The Entrepreneur's Perspective

Regardless of who your investors are, fight to have them vote as a single class. It's critical for your sanity. It keeps investors aligned. And as long as your capitalization table is rational, it won't matter.

Some investors feel they have enough control with their board involvement to ensure that the company does not take any action contrary to their interests, and as a result will not focus on these protective provisions. During a financing this is the typical argument used by company counsel to try to convince the VCs to back off of some or all of the protective provisions. We think this is a shortsighted approach for the investor, since, as a board member, an investor designee has legal duties to work in the best interests of the company. Sometimes the interests of the company and a particular class of shareholders diverge. Therefore, there can be times when an individual would legally have to approve something as a board member in the best interests of the company as a whole and not have a protective provision to fall back on as a shareholder. While this dynamic does not necessarily benefit the entrepreneur, it's good governance as it functionally separates the duties of a board member from those of a shareholder, shining a brighter light on an area of potential conflict.

While one could make the argument that protective provisions are at the core of the trust between a VC and an entrepreneur, we think that's a hollow and naive statement. When an entrepreneur asks, "Don't you trust me? Why do we need these things?" the simple answer is that it is not an issue of trust. Rather, we like to eliminate the discussion about who ultimately gets to make which decisions before we do a deal. Eliminating the ambiguity in roles, control, and rules of engagement is an important part of any financing, and the protective provisions cut to the heart of this.

Occasionally the protective provisions can help the entrepreneur, especially in an acquisition scenario. Since the investor can effectively block a sale of the company, this provides the entrepreneur with some addition leverage when negotiating with the buyer since the price needs to be high enough to garner the VC's consent on the deal. Of course, this assumes a reasonable position from the existing investor, but in most cases an experienced VC will support the entrepreneur's decision to sell a company.

A decade ago the protective provisions took several days to negotiate. Over time these provisions have been hotly tested in courts of law from several important judicial decisions, so today they have become mostly boilerplate.

The Entrepreneur's Perspective

Remember, you are negotiating this deal on behalf of the company (no matter who runs it in the future) and with the investors (no matter who owns the shares in the future). These terms are not only about your current relationship with the VC in question.

Drag-Along Agreement

Another important control provision is the *drag-along agreement*. Typical language follows:

> Drag-Along Agreement: The [holders of the Common Stock] or [Founders] and Series A Preferred shall enter into a drag-along agreement whereby if a majority of the holders of Series A Preferred agree to a sale or liquidation of the Company, the holders of the remaining Series A Preferred and Common Stock shall consent to and raise no objections to such sale.

The drag-along agreement gives a subset of the investors the ability to force, or drag along, all of the other investors and the founders to do a sale of the company, regardless of how the folks being dragged along feel about the deal.

After the Internet bubble burst and sales of companies started occurring that were at or below the liquidation preferences, entrepreneurs and founders—not surprisingly—started to resist selling the company in these situations since they often weren't getting anything in the deal. While there are several mechanisms to address sharing consideration below the liquidation preferences, such as the notion of a *carve-out*, which we'll discuss later, the fundamental issue is that if a transaction occurs below the liquidation preferences, it's likely that some or all of the VCs are losing money on the transaction. The VC point of view on this varies widely and is often dependent on the situation; some VCs can deal with this and are happy to provide some consideration to management to get a deal done, whereas others are stubborn in their view that since they lost money, management and founders shouldn't receive anything.

In each of these situations, the VCs would much rather control their ability to compel other shareholders to support the transaction. As more of these situations appeared, the major holders of common stock (even when they were in the minority of ownership) began refusing to vote for the proposed transaction unless the holders of preferred stock waived part of their liquidation preferences in favor of the common stock. Needless to say, this particular holdout technique did not go over well in the venture community and, as a result, the drag-along agreement became more prevalent.

If you are faced with a drag-along situation, your ownership position will determine whether or not this is an important issue for you. An acquisition does not require unanimous consent of shareholders; these rules vary by jurisdiction, although the two most common situations are either majority of each class (California) or majority of all shares on an as-converted basis (Delaware). However, most acquirers will want 85 percent to 90 percent of shareholders to consent to a transaction. If you own 1 percent of a company and the VCs would like you to sign up to a drag-along agreement, it doesn't matter that much unless there are 30 of you who each own 1 percent. Make sure you know what you are fighting for in the negotiation, and don't put disproportionate energy against terms that don't matter.

When a company is faced with a drag-along agreement in a VC financing proposal, the most common compromise position is to try to get the drag-along rights to pertain to following the majority of the common stock, not the preferred. This way, if you own common stock, you are dragged along only when a majority of the common stockholders consents to the transaction. This is a graceful position for a very small investor to take (e.g., "I'll play ball if a majority of the common plays ball") and one that we've always been willing to take when we've owned common stock in a company (e.g., "I'm not going to stand in the way of something a majority of folks who have rights equal to me want to do"). Of course, preferred investors can always convert some of their holdings to common stock to generate a majority, but this also results in a benefit to the common stockholders as it lowers the overall liquidation preference.

The Entrepreneur's Perspective

This is one of those terms that matter most if things are falling apart, in which case you probably have bigger fish to fry. And it cuts both ways—if you have a lot of investors, for example, this term can force them all to agree to a deal, which might save you from a lot of agitation down the road. Of course, it is best to not be in a fire sale situation, or at least to have enough board members whom you control (at least effectively, if not contractually) so that you can prevent a bad deal from happening in the first place.

Conversion

While many VCs posture during term sheet negotiations by saying things like "That is nonnegotiable," terms rarely are. Occasionally, though, a term will actually be nonnegotiable, and conversion is one such term.

The Entrepreneur's Perspective

Amen. "This is nonnegotiable" is usually a phrase thrown out by junior members of VC firms when they don't know any better. In particular, watch out for the "This is how we always do deals" or "This is a standard deal term for us" negotiating tactic as being ultra-lame and a sign that the people you're negotiating with don't really know what they are doing.

In all the VC deals we've ever seen, the preferred shareholders have the right—at any time—to convert their stake into common stock. Following is the standard language:

> Conversion: The holders of the Series A Preferred shall have the right to convert the Series A Preferred, at any time, into shares of Common Stock. The initial conversion rate shall be 1:1, subject to adjustment as provided below.

This allows the buyers of preferred to convert to common should they determine on a liquidation that they would be better off getting paid on an as-converted common basis rather than accepting the liquidation preference and the participation amount. It can also be used in certain extreme circumstances whereby the preferred wants to control a vote of the common on a certain issue. Note, however, that once converted, there is no provision for reconverting back to preferred.

A more interesting term is the automatic conversion, especially since it has several components that are negotiable.

> Automatic Conversion: All of the Series A Preferred shall be automatically converted into Common Stock, at the then applicable conversion price, upon the closing of a firmly underwritten public offering of shares of Common Stock of the Company at

a per share price not less than [three] times the Original Purchase Price (as adjusted for stock splits, dividends, and the like) per share and for a total offering of not less than [$15] million (before deduction of underwriters' commissions and expenses) (a "Qualified IPO"). All, or a portion of each share, of the Series A Preferred shall be automatically converted into Common Stock, at the then applicable conversion price in the event that the holders of at least a majority of the outstanding Series A Preferred consent to such conversion.

In an IPO of a venture-backed company, the investment bankers will almost always want to see everyone convert into common stock at the time of the IPO. It is rare for a venture-backed company to go public with multiple classes of stock, although occasionally you will see dual classes of shares in an IPO as Google had. The thresholds for the automatic conversion are critical to negotiate. As the entrepreneur you want them lower to ensure more flexibility, whereas your investors will want them higher to give them more control over the timing and terms of an IPO.

Regardless of the actual thresholds, it's important to never allow investors to negotiate different automatic conversion terms for different series of preferred stock. There are many horror stories of companies on the brink of going public with one class of preferred stockholders having a threshold above what the proposed offering would result in; as a result, these stockholders have an effective veto right on the offering.

For example, assume that you have an early stage investor with an automatic conversion threshold of $30 million and a later stage investor with an automatic conversion threshold of $60 million. Now, assume you are at the goal line for an IPO and it's turning out to be a $50 million offering based on the market and the demand for your company. Your early investor is ready to go, but your later stage investor suddenly says, "I'd like a little something else since I can block the deal and even though you've done all of this work to get to an IPO, I don't think I can support it unless. . . ." In these cases, much last-minute legal and financial wrangling ensues given the lack of alignment between your different classes of investors. To avoid this, we strongly recommend that you equalize the automatic conversion threshold among all series of stock at each financing.

The Entrepreneur's Perspective

Understand what the norms are for new IPOs before you dig your heels in on conversion terms. There's no reason to negotiate away other more critical terms over a $20 million threshold versus a $30 million threshold if the norm is $50 million. Besides, a board decision to pursue an IPO will put pressure on a VC to waive this provision.

CHAPTER

6

Other Terms of the Term Sheet

Up to this point we've been exploring terms that matter a lot and fall under the category of economics or control. As we get further into the term sheet, we start to encounter some terms that don't matter as much, are only impactful in a downside scenario, or don't matter at all.

This chapter covers those terms, which include dividends, redemption rights, conditions precedent to financing, information rights, registration rights, right of first refusal, voting rights, restriction on sales, proprietary information and inventions agreement, cosale agreement, founders' activities, initial public offering shares purchase, no-shop agreement, indemnification, and assignment.

Dividends

Whereas private equity guys love dividends, many venture capitalists, especially early stage ones, don't really care about them. In our experience, the VCs who do care about dividends either come from a private equity background or are focused on downside protection in larger deals.

Typical dividend language in a term sheet follows:

> Dividends: The holders of the Series A Preferred shall be entitled to receive [non]cumulative dividends in preference to any dividend on the Common Stock at the rate of [8 percent] of the Original Purchase Price per annum[, when and as declared by the Board of Directors]. The holders of Series A Preferred also

> shall be entitled to participate pro rata in any dividends paid on
> the Common Stock on an as-if-converted basis.

For early stage investments, dividends generally do not provide venture returns—they are simply additional juice in a deal. Let's do some simple math. Assume a typical dividend of 10 percent (dividends will range from 5 to 15 percent depending on how aggressive your investor is; we picked 10 percent to make the math easy).

Now, assume that the VC has negotiated hard and gotten a 10 percent cumulative annual dividend. In this case, the VC automatically gets the dividend every year. To keep the math simple, let's assume the dividend does not compound. As a result, each year the VC gets 10 percent of the investment as a dividend. Assume a home run deal such as a 50× return on a $10 million investment in five years. Even with a 10 percent cumulative annual dividend, this increases the VC's return from $500 million to only $505 million (the annual dividend is $1 million, or 10 percent of $10 million, times five years).

While the extra money from the dividend is nice, it doesn't really move the needle in the success case. Since venture funds typically have a 10-year life, the dividend generates another 1× return only if you invest on day one of a fund and hold the investment for 10 years.

This also assumes the company can actually pay out the dividend. Usually the dividends can be paid in either stock or cash, typically at the option of the company. Obviously, the dividend could drive additional dilution if it is paid out in stock, so this is the one case in which it is important not to get head-faked by the investor, where the dividend becomes another form of antidilution protection—one that is automatic and simply linked to the passage of time.

We are being optimistic about the return scenarios. In downside cases, the dividend can matter, especially as the invested capital increases. For example, take a $40 million investment with a 10 percent annual cumulative dividend in a company that was sold at the end of the fifth year to another company for $80 million. In this case, assume that there was a simple liquidation preference with no participation and the investor got 40 percent of the company for his investment (at a $100 million postmoney valuation). Since the sale price was below the investment postmoney valuation (i.e., a loser, but not a disaster), the investor will exercise the liquidation preference and take the $40 million plus the dividend ($4 million per year for five years, or $20 million). In this case, the difference between the return in a no-dividend scenario ($40 million) and a dividend scenario ($60 million) is material.

Mathematically, the larger the investment amount and the lower the expected exit multiple, the more the dividend matters. This is why you see dividends in private equity and buyout deals where big money is involved (typically greater than $50 million) and the expectation for return multiples on invested capital is lower.

Automatic dividends have some nasty side effects, especially if the company runs into trouble, since they typically should be included in the solvency analysis. If you aren't paying attention, an automatic cumulative dividend can put you unknowingly into the *zone of insolvency*, which is a bad place to be. Cumulative dividends can also be an accounting nightmare, especially when they are optionally paid in stock, cash, or a conversion adjustment, but that's why the accountants get paid the big bucks at the end of the year to put together the audited balance sheet.

That said, the noncumulative dividend when declared by the board is benign, rarely declared, and an artifact of the past, so we typically leave it in term sheets just to give the lawyers something to do.

The Entrepreneur's Perspective

The thing to care about here is ensuring that dividends have to be approved by a majority—or even a supermajority—of your board of directors.

Redemption Rights

Even though redemption rights rarely come into play, many VCs are often overly focused on them in the deal because they provide additional downside protection. A typical redemption rights clause follows:

> Redemption at Option of Investors: At the election of the holders of at least a majority of the Series A Preferred, the Company shall redeem the outstanding Series A Preferred in three annual installments beginning on the [fifth] anniversary of the

Closing. Such redemptions shall be at a purchase price equal to the Original Purchase Price plus declared and unpaid dividends.

There is some rationale for redemption rights. First, there is the fear (on the VC's part) that a company will become successful enough to be an ongoing business but not quite successful enough to go public or be acquired. In this case, redemption rights were invented to allow the investor a guaranteed exit path. However, a company that is around for a while as a going concern while not being an attractive initial public offering (IPO) or acquisition candidate generally won't have the cash to pay out redemption rights.

Another reason for redemption rights pertains to the life span of venture funds. The average venture fund has a 10-year life span to conduct its business. If a VC makes an investment in year five of the fund, it might be important for that fund manager to secure redemption rights in order to have a liquidity path before the fund must wind down. As with the previous case, whether or not the company has the ability to pay is another matter.

Often, companies will claim that redemption rights create a liability on their balance sheet and can make certain business optics more difficult. By optics, we mean how certain third-parties view the health and stability of the company such as bankers, customers and employees. In the past few years, accountants have begun to argue more strongly that redeemable preferred stock is a liability on the balance sheet, not an equity feature. Unless the redeemable preferred stock is mandatorily redeemable, this is not the case, and most experienced accountants will be able to recognize the difference.

There is one form of redemption that we have seen in the past few years that we view as overreaching—the *adverse change redemption*. We recommend you never agree to the following term that has recently crept into term sheets:

Adverse Change Redemption: Should the Company experience a material adverse change to its prospects, business, or financial position, the holders of at least a majority of the Series A Preferred shall have the option to commit the Company to immediately redeem the outstanding Series A Preferred. Such redemption shall be at a purchase price equal to the Original Purchase Price plus declared and unpaid dividends.

This term effectively gives the VC a right to a redemption in the case of a "material adverse change to its . . . business." The problem is that "material adverse change" is not defined, is a vague concept, is too punitive, and shifts an inappropriate amount of control to the investors based on an arbitrary judgment of the investors. If this term is being proposed and you are getting resistance on eliminating it, make sure you are speaking to a professional investor and not a loan shark.

In our experience, redemption rights are well understood by VCs and should not create a problem, except in a theoretical argument between lawyers and accountants.

The Entrepreneur's Perspective

I don't worry about redemption rights much, although the adverse change redemption clause is evil. As with dividends, just make sure you have maximum protection around your board, or all classes of preferred shareholders voting in aggregate, and not just the majority of a random class of shareholder declaring these.

Conditions Precedent to Financing

While there is a lot to negotiate, a term sheet is simply a step on the way to an actual deal. Term sheets are often nonbinding (or mostly nonbinding) and most VCs will load them up with conditions precedent to financing. Entrepreneurs glance over these, usually because they are in the back sections of the term sheet and seem pretty innocuous, but they occasionally have additional ways out of a deal for the investor that the entrepreneur should watch for, if only to better understand the current mind-set of the investor proposing the investment.

A typical conditions precedent to financing clause looks like this:

> Conditions Precedent to Financing: Except for the provisions contained herein entitled "Legal Fees and Expenses," "No-Shop Agreement," and "Governing Law," which are explicitly agreed by the Investors and the Company to be binding upon execution of this term sheet, this summary of terms is not intended as a legally binding commitment by the Investors, and any obligation

on the part of the Investors is subject to the following conditions precedent: 1. Completion of legal documentation satisfactory to the prospective Investors; 2. Satisfactory completion of due diligence by the prospective Investors; 3. Delivery of a customary management rights letter to Investors; and 4. Submission of a detailed budget for the following twelve (12) months, acceptable to Investors.

Note that the investors will try to make a few things binding—specifically that legal fees get paid whether or not a deal happens, the company can't shop the deal once the term sheet is signed, or the governing law be set to a specific domicile—while explicitly stating that a bunch things still have to happen before this deal is done, and they can back out for any reason.

The Entrepreneur's Perspective

Try to avoid conditions precedent to financing as much as possible. Again, the best Plan A has the strongest Plan B standing behind it. Your prospective VC should be willing to move quickly and snap up your deal on acceptable terms by the time the VC gets to a term sheet. At a minimum, do not agree to pay for the VC's legal fees unless the deal is completed (with a possible carve-out for you canceling the deal).

There are three conditions to watch out for since they usually signal something nonobvious on the part of the VC. They are:

1. *Approval by investors' partnerships.* This is secret VC code for "This deal has not been approved by the investors who issued this term sheet." Therefore, even if you love the terms of the deal, you still may not have a deal.
2. *Rights offering to be completed by company.* This indicates that the VCs want to offer all previous investors in the company the ability to participate in the currently contemplated financing. This is not necessarily a bad thing, as in most cases it serves to protect all parties from liability, but it does add time and expense to the deal.

3. *Employment agreements signed by founders as acceptable to investors.* Be aware of what the full terms are before signing the agreement. As an entrepreneur, when faced with this, it's probably wise to understand and negotiate the form of employment agreement early in the process. You'll want to try to do this before you sign a term sheet and accept a no-shop clause, but most VCs will wave you off and say, "Don't worry about it—we'll come up with something that works for everyone." Make sure you understand the key terms such as compensation and what happens if you get fired.

The Entrepreneur's Perspective

Insist on spelling out key terms prior to a signed term sheet if it has a no-shop clause in it. A VC who won't spell out key employment terms at the beginning is a big red flag.

There are plenty of other wacky conditions—if you can dream it up, it has probably been done. Just make sure to look carefully at this paragraph and remember that you don't necessarily have a deal just because you've signed a term sheet.

Information Rights

We are back to another ubiquitous term that is important to the VC but shouldn't matter much to the entrepreneur. Information rights define the type of information the VC legally has access to and the time frame in which the company is required to deliver it to the VC.

Information Rights: So long as an Investor continues to hold [any] shares of Series A Preferred or Common Stock issued upon conversion of the Series A Preferred, the Company shall deliver to the Investor the Company's annual budget, as well as audited annual and unaudited quarterly financial statements. Furthermore, as soon as reasonably possible, the Company shall furnish a report to each Investor comparing each annual budget to such financial statements. Each Investor shall also be entitled to standard inspection and visitation rights. These provisions shall terminate upon a Qualified IPO.

You might ask, "If these terms rarely matter, why bother?" Since you will end up having to deal with them in a VC term sheet, you might as well be exposed to them and hear that they don't matter much. Of course, from a VC perspective, "doesn't matter much" can also mean "Mr. Entrepreneur, please don't pay much attention to these terms—just accept them as is." However, our view is that if an investor or the company is hotly negotiating this particular term, that time (and lawyer money) is most likely being wasted.

Information rights are generally something companies are stuck with in order to get investment capital. The only variation one sees is putting a threshold on the number of shares held (some finite number versus "any") for investors to continue to enjoy these rights.

The Entrepreneur's Perspective

If you care about information rights for your shareholders, you are nuts. You should run a transparent organization as much as possible in the twenty-first century. If you can't commit to sending your shareholders a budget and financial statements, you shouldn't take on outside investors. If you are of the paranoid mind-set (which I generally applaud), feel free to insist on a strict confidentiality clause to accompany your information rights.

Registration Rights

Registration rights define the rights that investors have to registering their shares in an IPO scenario as well as the obligation of the company to the VCs whenever they file additional registration statements after the IPO. This is a tedious example of something that rarely matters, yet tends to take up a page or more of the term sheet. Get ready for your mind to be numbed.

> Registration Rights: Demand Rights: If Investors holding more than 50 percent of the outstanding shares of Series A Preferred, including Common Stock issued on conversion of Series A Preferred ("Registrable Securities"), or a lesser percentage if the anticipated aggregate offering price to the public is not less than $5,000,000, request that the Company file a Registration Statement, the Company will use its best efforts to cause such shares to be registered; provided, however, that the Company shall not

be obligated to effect any such registration prior to the [third] anniversary of the Closing. The Company shall have the right to delay such registration under certain circumstances for one period not in excess of ninety (90) days in any twelve (12)-month period.

The Company shall not be obligated to effect more than two (2) registrations under these demand right provisions, and shall not be obligated to effect a registration (i) during the one hundred eighty (180)-day period commencing with the date of the Company's initial public offering, or (ii) if it delivers notice to the holders of the Registrable Securities within thirty (30) days of any registration request of its intent to file a registration statement for such initial public offering within ninety (90) days.

Company Registration: The Investors shall be entitled to "piggyback" registration rights on all registrations of the Company or on any demand registrations of any other investor subject to the right, however, of the Company and its underwriters to reduce the number of shares proposed to be registered pro rata in view of market conditions. If the Investors are so limited, however, no party shall sell shares in such registration other than the Company or the Investor, if any, invoking the demand registration. Unless the registration is with respect to the Company's initial public offering, in no event shall the shares to be sold by the Investors be reduced below 30 percent of the total amount of securities included in the registration. No shareholder of the Company shall be granted piggyback registration rights which would reduce the number of shares includable by the holders of the Registrable Securities in such registration without the consent of the holders of at least a majority of the Registrable Securities.

S-3 Rights: Investors shall be entitled to unlimited demand registrations on Form S-3 (if available to the Company) so long as such registered offerings are not less than $1,000,000.

Expenses: The Company shall bear registration expenses (exclusive of underwriting discounts and commissions) of all such demands, piggybacks, and S-3 registrations (including the expense of one special counsel of the selling shareholders not to exceed $25,000).

Transfer of Rights: The registration rights may be transferred to (i) any partner, member, or retired partner or member or affiliated fund of any holder which is a partnership, (ii) any member or former member of any holder which is a limited liability company, (iii) any family member or trust for the benefit of any individual holder, or (iv) any transferee who satisfies the criteria to be a Major Investor (as defined below); provided the Company is given written notice thereof.

Lockup Provision: Each Investor agrees that it will not sell its shares for a period to be specified by the managing underwriter (but not to exceed 180 days) following the effective date of the Company's initial public offering; provided that all officers, directors, and other 1 percent shareholders are similarly bound. Such lockup agreement shall provide that any discretionary waiver or termination of the restrictions of such agreements by the Company or representatives of underwriters shall apply to Major Investors, pro rata, based on the number of shares held.

Other Provisions: Other provisions shall be contained in the Investor Rights Agreement with respect to registration rights as are reasonable, including cross-indemnification, the period of time in which the Registration Statement shall be kept effective, and underwriting arrangements. The Company shall not require the opinion of Investor's counsel before authorizing the transfer of stock or the removal of Rule 144 legends for routine sales under Rule 144 or for distribution to partners or members of Investors.

Registration rights are something the company will almost always have to offer to investors. What is most interesting about registration rights is that lawyers seem genetically incapable of leaving this section untouched and always end up negotiating something. Perhaps because this provision is so long, they feel the need to keep their pens warm while reading. We find it humorous (as long as we aren't the ones paying the legal fees), because in the end, the modifications are generally innocuous, and besides, if you ever get to the point where registration rights come into play (e.g., an IPO), the investment bankers of the company are going to have a major hand in deciding how the deal is going to be structured, regardless of the contract the company entered into years before when it did an early stage financing.

The Entrepreneur's Perspective

Don't focus much energy on registration rights. This is more about upside. The world is good if you're going public.

Right of First Refusal

The right of first refusal defines the rights that an investor has to buy shares in a future financing. Right of first refusal is another chewy term that takes up a lot of space in the term sheet but is hard for the entrepreneur to have much impact on. Following is the typical language.

> Right of First Refusal: Investors who purchase at least ___ shares of Series A Preferred (a "Major Investor") shall have the right in the event the Company proposes to offer equity securities to any person, other than the shares (i) reserved as employee shares described under "Employee Pool" below; (ii) shares issued for consideration other than cash pursuant to a merger, consolidation, acquisition, or similar business combination approved by the Board; (iii) shares issued pursuant to any equipment loan or leasing arrangement, real property leasing arrangement, or debt financing from a bank or similar financial institution approved by the Board; and (iv) shares with respect to which the holders of a majority of the outstanding Series A Preferred waive their right of first refusal, to purchase [X] times their pro rata portion of such shares. Any securities not subscribed for by an eligible Investor may be reallocated among the other eligible Investors. Such right of first refusal will terminate upon a Qualified IPO. For purposes of this right of first refusal, an Investor's pro rata right shall be equal to the ratio of (a) the number of shares of common stock (including all shares of common stock issuable or issued upon the conversion of convertible securities and assuming the exercise of all outstanding warrants and options) held by such Investor immediately prior to the issuance of such

equity securities to (b) the total number of share of common stock outstanding (including all shares of common stock issuable or issued upon the conversion of convertible securities and assuming the exercise of all outstanding warrants and options) immediately prior to the issuance of such equity securities.

The right of first refusal is also known as a *pro rata right*. While almost all VCs will insist on a right of first refusal, there are two things to pay attention to in this term that can be negotiated. First, the share threshold that defines a *major investor* can be defined. It's often convenient, especially if you have a large number of small investors, not to have to give this right to them. However, since in future rounds you are typically interested in getting as much participation from your existing investors as you can, it's not worth struggling with this too much.

A more important thing to look for is to see if there is a multiple on the purchase rights (e.g., the "[X] times" listed). This is often referred to as a *super pro rata right* and is an excessive ask, especially early in the financing life cycle of a company.

The Entrepreneur's Perspective

The right of first refusal is not a big deal, and in some cases it's good for you. But make sure you define what a major investor is and give this only to them. At a minimum, you can make sure that shareholders get this right only if they play in subsequent rounds.

Voting Rights

Voting rights define how the preferred stock and the common stock relate to each other in the context of a share vote. It is another term that doesn't matter that much. The typical language follows:

Voting Rights: The Series A Preferred will vote together with the Common Stock and not as a separate class except as specifically provided herein or as otherwise required by law. The Common Stock may be increased or decreased by the vote of holders of a majority of the Common Stock and Series A Preferred voting together on an as-if-converted basis, and without a separate class vote. Each share of Series A Preferred shall have a number of votes equal to the number of shares of Common Stock then issuable upon conversion of such share of Series A Preferred.

Most of the time the voting rights clause is simply an FYI section, as all the important rights, such as the protective provisions, are contained in other sections.

Restriction on Sales

The restriction on sales clause, also known as the right of first refusal on sales of common stock (or ROFR on common) defines the parameters associated with selling shares of stock when the company is a private company. Typical language follows:

> Restrictions on Sales: The Company's Bylaws shall contain a right of first refusal on all transfers of Common Stock, subject to normal exceptions. If the Company elects not to exercise its right, the Company shall assign its right to the Investors.

Historically, founders and management rarely argue against this, as it helps control the shareholder base of the company, which usually benefits all the existing shareholders (except possibly the ones who want to bail out of their private stock). However, we've found that the lawyers will often spend time arguing about how to implement this particular clause—specifically whether to include it in the bylaws or include it in each of the company's option agreements, plans, and stock sales. We find it easier to include this clause in the bylaws since then it's in one place and is hard to overlook.

In the early days of venture capital (say, until 2007) there was a strong conventional wisdom that founders and management shouldn't be able to sell their shares until the investors could sell their shares, through either an IPO or a sale of the company. As the time to liquidity for private companies stretched out and IPOs became less common, this philosophy shifted. Simultaneously, a healthy secondary market for founders and early employee shares appeared, fueled both by the rapid rise in valuation of private companies such as Facebook and Twitter, along with the emergence of private secondary markets such as Second Market and SharesPost. The result is a lot more sales of private stock to other investors (sometimes new ones, sometimes the existing investors) along with much more scrutiny and discussion around the ROFR on common construct.

After being involved in several situations where this has come into play, we feel more strongly than ever that an ROFR on common is a good thing for the company and should be supported by the founders, management, and investors. Controlling the share ownership in a private company is important, especially as the Securities and Exchange Commission (SEC) takes a closer look at various private shareholder rules—both regarding ownership and for stock sales. The ROFR on common gives the company the ability to at least know what is going on and make decisions in the context of the various proposals.

Proprietary Information and Inventions Agreement

Every term sheet we've ever seen has a proprietary information and inventions agreement clause.

> Proprietary Information and Inventions Agreement: Each current and former officer, employee, and consultant of the Company shall enter into an acceptable proprietary information and inventions agreement.

This paragraph benefits both the company and investors and is simply a mechanism that investors use to get the company to legally stand behind the representation that it owns its intellectual property (IP). Many pre–Series A companies have issues surrounding this, especially if the company hasn't had great legal representation prior to its first venture round. We've also run into plenty of situations (including several of ours—oops!) in which companies are loose about this between financings and, while a financing is a good time to clean this up, it's often annoying to previously hired employees who are now told, "Hey—you need to sign this since we need it for the venture financing." It's even more important in the sale of a company, as the buyer will always insist on clear ownership of the IP. Our best advice here is that companies should build these agreements into their hiring process from the very beginning (with the advice from a good law firm) so that there are never any issues around this, as VCs will always insist on this agreement.

The Entrepreneur's Perspective

A proprietary information and inventions agreement clause is good for the company. You should have all employees, including founders, sign something like this before you do an outside venture financing. If someone on the team needs a specific carve-out for work in progress that is unrelated to the business, you and your investors should be willing to grant it.

Co-Sale Agreement

Most investors will insist on a co-sale agreement, which states that if a founder sells shares, the investors will have an opportunity to sell a proportional amount of their stock as well. Typical language follows:

> Co-Sale Agreement: The shares of the Company's securities held by the Founders shall be made subject to a co-sale agreement (with certain reasonable exceptions) with the Investors such that the Founders may not sell, transfer, or exchange their stock unless each Investor has an opportunity to participate in the sale on a pro rata basis. This right of co-sale shall not apply to and shall terminate upon a Qualified IPO.

The chance of keeping this provision out of a financing is close to zero, so we don't think it's worth fighting it. Notice that this matters only while the company is private—if the company goes public, this clause no longer applies.

The Entrepreneur's Perspective

Your chances of eliminating the co-sale agreement clause may be zero, but there's no reason not to ask for a floor to it. If you or your co-founders want to sell a small amount of stock to buy a house, why should a VC hold it up? A right of first refusal on the purchase with a bona fide outside offer's valuation as the purchase price is one thing. An effective exclusion is something entirely different.

Founders' Activities

As you wind your way through a typical term sheet, you'll often see, buried near the back, a short clause concerning founders' activities. It usually looks something like this:

> Founders' Activities: Each of the Founders shall devote 100 percent of his professional time to the Company. Any other professional activities will require the approval of the Board of Directors.

It should be no surprise to a founder that your friendly neighborhood VC wants you to be spending 100 percent (actually 120 percent) of your time and attention on your company. If this paragraph sneaks its way into the term sheet, the VC either has recently been burned, is suspicious, or is concerned that one or more of the founders may be working on something besides the company being funded.

Of course, this is a classic no-win situation for a founder. If you are actually working on something else at the same time and don't disclose it, you are violating the terms of the agreement in addition to breaching trust before you get started. If you do disclose other activities or push back on this clause (hence signaling that you are working on something else), you'll reinforce the concern that the VC has. So tread carefully here. Our recommendation, unless of course you are working on something else, is simply to agree to this.

In situations where we've worked with a founder who already has other obligations or commitments, we've always appreciated him being up front with us early in the process. We've usually been able to work through these situations in a way that results in everyone being happy and, in the cases where we couldn't get there, were glad that the issue came up early so that we didn't waste our time or the entrepreneur's time.

While there are situations where VCs get comfortable with entrepreneurs working on multiple companies simultaneously (usually with very experienced entrepreneurs or in situations where the VC and the entrepreneur have worked together in the past), they are the exception, not the norm.

The Entrepreneur's Perspective

If you can't agree to a founders' activities clause, don't look for professional VC financing. Or you can negotiate a very specific carve-out, and expect other consequences in your terms (e.g., vesting and IP rights).

Initial Public Offering Shares Purchase

One of the terms that falls into the "nice problem to have" category is the initial public offering shares purchase.

> Initial Public Offering Shares Purchase: In the event that the Company shall consummate a Qualified IPO, the Company shall use its best efforts to cause the managing underwriter or underwriters of such IPO to offer to [investors] the right to purchase at least [5 percent] of any shares issued under a "friends and family" or "directed shares" program in connection with such Qualified IPO. Notwithstanding the foregoing, all action taken pursuant to this Section shall be made in accordance with all federal and state securities laws, including, without limitation, Rule 134 of the Securities Act of 1933, as amended, and all applicable rules and regulations promulgated by the National Association of Securities Dealers, Inc. and other such self-regulating organizations.

This term blossomed in the late 1990s when anything that was VC funded was positioned as a company that would shortly go public. However, most investment bankers will push back on this term if the IPO is going to be a success, as they want to get stock into the hands of institutional investors (their clients). If the VCs get this push-back, they are usually so giddy with joy that the company is going public that they don't argue with the bankers. Ironically, if they don't get this push-back, or even worse, get a call near the end of the IPO road show in which the bankers are asking them to buy shares in the offering, they usually panic and do whatever they can to not have to buy into the offering since this means the deal is no longer a hot one.

Our recommendation on this one is don't worry about it or spend lawyer time on it.

No-Shop Agreement

As an entrepreneur, the way to get the best deal for a round of financing is to have multiple options. However, there comes a point in time when you have to choose your investor and shift from "search for an investor" mode to "close the deal" mode. Part of this involves choosing your lead investor and negotiating the final term sheet with him.

A no-shop agreement is almost always part of this final term sheet. Think of it as serial monogamy—your new investor-to-be doesn't want you running around behind his back just as you are about to get hitched. A typical no-shop agreement follows:

> No-Shop Agreement: The Company agrees to work in good faith expeditiously toward a closing. The Company and the Founders agree that they will not, directly or indirectly, (i) take any action to solicit, initiate, encourage, or assist the submission of any proposal, negotiation, or offer from any person or entity other than the Investors relating to the sale or issuance of any of the capital stock of the Company or the acquisition, sale, lease, license, or other disposition of the Company or any material part of the stock or assets of the Company, or (ii) enter into any discussions or negotiations or execute any agreement related to any of the foregoing, and shall notify the Investors promptly of any inquiries by any third parties in regard to the foregoing. Should both parties agree that definitive documents shall not be executed pursuant to this term sheet, then the Company shall have no further obligations under this section.

At some level the no-shop agreement, like serial monogamy, is more of an emotional commitment than a legal one. While it's very hard, but not impossible, to enforce a no-shop agreement in a financing, if you get caught cheating, your financing will probably go the same way as the analogous situation when the groom or the bride-to-be gets caught in a compromising situation.

The no-shop agreement reinforces the handshake that says, "Okay, let's get a deal done—no more fooling around looking for a better or different one." In all cases, the entrepreneur should bound the no-shop agreement by a time period—usually 45 to 60 days is plenty, although you can occasionally get a VC to agree to a 30-day no-shop agreement. This makes the commitment bidirectional—you agree not to shop the deal; the VC agrees to get things done within a reasonable time frame.

Now, some entrepreneurs still view that as a unilateral agreement; namely, the entrepreneur is agreeing to the no-shop but the VC isn't really agreeing to anything at all. In most cases, we don't view the no-shop clause as terribly important since it can be bounded with time. Instead, we feel it's much more important for the entrepreneur to test the VCs commitment to follow through on the investment when signing up to do the deal.

Specifically, in some cases VCs put down term sheets early, well before they've got internal agreement within their partnership to do an investment. This used to be more common; today many early stage VCs don't want to go through the hassle of drafting the term sheet and trying to negotiate it unless they believe they will do the deal. In addition, there is a potential negative reputational impact for the VC, as word will get around that VC X puts term sheets out early, but then can't or won't close. In the age of the Internet, this type of reputation spreads like an infectious disease.

Although we've done hundreds of investments, we came up with only a few examples in the past 15 years where the no-shop agreement had any meaningful impact on a deal in which we were involved. When we thought about the situations in which we were the VC and were negatively impacted by not having a no-shop agreement (e.g., a company we had agreed with on a term sheet went and did something else) or where we were on the receiving end of a no-shop agreement and were negatively impacted by it (e.g., an acquirer tied us up but then ultimately didn't close on the deal), we actually didn't feel particularly bad about any of the situations since there were both logic associated with the outcome and grace exhibited by the participants. Following are two examples:

We signed a term sheet to invest in Company X. We didn't include a no-shop clause in the term sheet. We were working to close the investment (we were 15 days into a 30-ish-day process) and had legal documents going back and forth. One of the founders called us and said that they had just received an offer to be acquired and they wanted to pursue it. We told them no problem—we'd still be there to do the deal if it didn't come together. We were very open with them about the pros and cons of doing the deal from our perspective and, given the economics, encouraged them to pursue the acquisition offer (it was a great deal for them). They ended up closing the deal and, as a token, gave us a small amount of equity in the company for our efforts (totally unexpected and unnecessary, but appreciated).

In another situation we were already investors in a company that was in the process of closing an outside-led round at a significant step-up in valuation. The company was under a no-shop agreement with the new VC. A week prior to closing, we received an acquisition overture from one of the strategic investors in the company. We immediately told the new lead investor about it, who graciously agreed to suspend the no-shop agreement and wait to see whether we wanted to move forward with the acquisition or with the financing. We negotiated with the acquirer for several weeks, checking regularly with the new potential investor to make sure they were still interested in closing the round if we chose not to pursue the acquisition. They were incredibly supportive and patient. The company covered its legal fees up to that point (unprompted—although it was probably in the term sheet that we'd cover them; we can't recall). We ended up moving forward with the acquisition; the new investor was disappointed in the outcome but happy and supportive of what we did.

While both of these are edge cases, in almost all of our experiences the no-shop agreement ended up being irrelevant. As each of these examples shows, the quality and the character of the people involved made all the difference and were much more important than the legal term.

The Entrepreneur's Perspective

As an entrepreneur, you should also ask that the no-shop clause expire immediately if the VC terminates the process. Also, consider asking for a carve-out for acquisitions. Frequently financings and acquisitions follow each other around. Even if you're not looking to be acquired, you don't want handcuffs on conversations about an acquisition just because a VC is negotiating with you about a financing.

Indemnification

The indemnification clause states that the company will indemnify investors and board members to the maximum extent possible by law. It is another one that entrepreneurs just have to live with. It follows:

> Indemnification: The bylaws and/or other charter documents of the Company shall limit board members' liability and exposure to damages to the broadest extent permitted by applicable law. The Company will indemnify board members and will indemnify each Investor for any claims brought against the Investors by any third party (including any other shareholder of the Company) as a result of this financing.

Given all the shareholder litigation in recent years, there is almost no chance that a company will get funded without indemnifying its directors. The first sentence is simply a contractual obligation between the company and its board. The second sentence, which is occasionally negotiable, indicates the desire for the company to purchase formal liability insurance. One can usually negotiate away insurance in a Series A deal, but for any follow-on financing the major practice today is to procure directors' and officers' (D&O) insurance. We believe companies should be willing to indemnify their directors and will likely need to purchase D&O insurance in order to attract outside board members.

The Entrepreneur's Perspective

You should have reasonable and customary directors' and officers' (D&O) insurance for yourself as much as for your VCs. While the indemnification clause is good corporate hygiene, make sure you follow it up with an appropriate insurance policy.

Assignment

We end this chapter with the assignment clause, another clause in a typical term sheet that isn't worth spending legal time and money negotiating.

Assignment: Each of the Investors shall be entitled to transfer all or part of its shares of Series A Preferred purchased by it to one or more affiliated partnerships or funds managed by it or any of their respective directors, officers, or partners, provided such transferee agrees in writing to be subject to the terms of the Stock Purchase Agreement and related agreements as if it were a purchaser thereunder.

The assignment clause simply gives VC firms flexibility over transfers that they require to be able to run their business and, as long as the VC is willing to require that any transferee agree to be subject to the various financing agreements, the company should be willing to provide for this. However, watch out for one thing—don't let the loophole "assignment without transfer of the obligation under the agreements" occur. You need to make sure that anyone who is on the receiving end of a transfer abides by the same rules and conditions that the original purchasers of the stock signed up for.

CHAPTER

7

The Capitalization Table

Now that we've worked through all of the specific clauses in the term sheet, let's go through how a typical *capitalization table* (*cap table*) works. A term sheet will almost always contain a summary cap table, which we describe in this chapter. You, your prospective investors, or occasionally your lawyers will generate a more detailed cap table.

The cap table summarizes who owns what part of the company before and after the financing. This is one area that some founders, especially those who have not been exposed in the past to cap table math, are often uncomfortable with. It's extremely important for founders to understand exactly who owns what part of a company and what the implications are in a potential funding round.

Normally when you initially set up the company, 100 percent will be allocated to the founders and employees, with a specific number of shares allocated to each individual. The question "What will I own if a VC invests X in my company at a Y valuation?" is rarely simple. To answer it, you need to be able to generate a cap table to truly analyze the deal presented by a particular term sheet. Following is a model to work from with a typical example.

Let's assume the following:

2,000,000 shares held by founders before the VC invests

$10 million premoney valuation

$5 million investment by the VC

In this example, the postmoney valuation is $15 million ($10 million premoney + $5 million investment). Consequently, the VCs own

33.33 percent of the company after the financing ($5 million investment/$15 million postmoney valuation). This should be pretty straightforward so far.

Now, assume the term sheet includes a new employee option pool of 20 percent on a postmoney basis. Remember that this means that after the financing, there will be an unallocated option pool equal to 20 percent of the company.

Although the postmoney valuation remains the same ($15 million), the requirement for a 20 percent option pool will have a significant impact on the ownership of the founders. Per the cap table, you can see how we calculate the percentage ownership for each class of owner, along with the price per share of the preferred stock. To start, we've filled in the known numbers and now have to solve for the unknowns (A, B, C, D, and E).

Example Capitalization Table

Class	Shares	Preferred Price	Valuation	Percentage
Founders	2,000,000			A
Employee pool	B			20%
Venture investors	C	D	$5,000,000	33.33%
Total	E	D	$15,000,000	100%

First, let's solve for A, the founders' ownership percentage: $A = 100$ percent minus the VC percentage minus the employee pool percentage, or $100\% - 33.33\% - 20\% = 46.67\%$. Given that we know that the 2,000,000 founders' shares represent 46.67 percent of the company, we can determine that the total shares outstanding ($E = 2,000,000/0.4667$) are 4,285,408. Now, if there are 4,285,408 shares outstanding, determining the number of shares in the employee pool becomes $B = E * 0.20$ or 857,081.

The same math applies for C, the number of shares of preferred stock the VCs have. $C = E * 0.3333$ or 1,428,326. Since $5 million bought 1,428,326 shares of preferred stock, then the price per share of preferred stock ($D = \$5,000,000/1,428,326$) is $3.50 per share.

Finally, always check your calculation. Since we know we have a $10 million premoney valuation, then the shares prior to the financing (2,000,000 founders' shares plus the 20 percent option pool) times the price per share should equal $10 million. If you do this math, you'll see that $(2,000,000 + 857,081) * \$3.50 = \$9,999,783.50$.

Oops, we are off by $216.50, which represents 62 shares (well, 61.857 shares).

While this is close enough for an example, it's not close enough for most VCs, or for most lawyers for that matter. And it shouldn't be close enough for you. That's why most cap tables have two additional significant digits (or fractional shares)—the rounding to the nearest share doesn't happen during intermediate steps, but only at the very end.

As the entrepreneur, you shouldn't blindly rely on legal counsel to generate these documents. There are a lot of good lawyers out there with poor math skills, and the cap table can get messed up when left in the hands of the lawyers. Although some get it right, it's your responsibility as the entrepreneur to make sure you understand your cap table. This will be especially helpful at times when you want to expand the employee option pool and you are eloquent in front of your board of directors explaining the ramifications.

The Entrepreneur's Perspective

If you do not have a great financially oriented founder, find someone who knows what he's doing to help you with the cap table—not just someone who knows math (a good starting point!), but someone who knows cap tables and VC financings.

CHAPTER 8

Convertible Debt

In the past few chapters we've gone through, in detail, the terms in a typical venture capital (VC) equity financing. However, there is one other type of financing, often used at the seed stage, called a convertible debt financing. In fact, many angel investors will invest only with this structure.

Convertible debt is just that: debt. It's a loan. The loan will convert to equity (preferred stock, usually) at such time as another round is raised. The conversion usually includes some sort of discount on the price to the future round.

For example, assume you raise $500,000 in convertible debt from angels with a 20 percent discount to the next round, and six months later a VC offers to lead a Series A round of a $1 million investment at $1.00 a share. Your financing will actually be for $1.5 million total, although the VCs will get 1 million Series A shares ($1 million at $1.00 per share) and the angels will get 625,000 Series A shares ($500,000 at $0.80 per share). The discount is appropriate, as your early investors want some reward for investing before the full Series A financing round comes together.

In this chapter, we cover the arguments for and against using convertible debt. We then go through the terms in a convertible debt deal, including the discount, valuation caps, interest rate, conversion mechanics, conversion in a sale of the company, warrants, and other terms. We briefly cover the differences between early stage and late stage dynamics and finish up with an example of when convertible debt could be dangerous to use.

Arguments For and Against Convertible Debt

Most fans of convertible debt argue that it's a much easier transaction to complete than an equity financing. Since no valuation is being set for the company, you get to avoid that part of the negotiation. Because it is debt, it has few, if any, of the rights of preferred stock offerings and you can accomplish a transaction with a lot less paperwork and legal fees. Note, however, that the legal fees argument is less persuasive these days with the many forms of standardized documents. A decade ago there could be a $50,000 pricing difference for legal fees between a seed preferred round and a convertible debt round. These days the difference is less than $10,000 since many lawyers will heavily discount the seed preferred round to get future business from the company.

The debate goes on endlessly about which structure is better or worse for entrepreneurs or investors. We aren't convinced there is a definitive answer here; in fact, we are convinced that those who think there is a definitive answer are wrong.

Since investors usually drive the decision about whether to raise an equity or a debt round, let's look at their motivations first. One of the primary reasons for an early stage investor to purchase equity is to price the stock being sold in the round. Early stage investing is a risky proposition, and investors will want to invest at low prices, although smart investors won't invest at a price at which founders are demotivated. As a result, most early stage deals get priced in a pretty tight range.

With a convertible debt structure, the stock price is not set and is determined at a later date when a larger financing occurs. By definition, if there is a later round the company must be doing something right. Having a discount is nice, but the ultimate price for the early convertible debt investors may still be higher than what they would have paid if they had bought equity in the first place. Some investors try to fix this problem by setting a cap on the price they will pay in the next round. In other words, as an investor, I'll take a 20 percent discount on the price of the next round up to a valuation of $X. If you get a valuation above $X, then my valuation is $X (hence the notion of a valuation cap).

This sounds like it fixes the problem, right? This might for the original investor, but it might not for the company and the founders. First of all, the investors coming into the next round may not like the idea that they are paying that much more than the convertible debt investors paid. Unlike equity, which is issued and can't be changed, the new equity investors could refuse to fund unless the debt investors remove or change the cap. Keep in mind that VCs will normally focus and peg their valuation of your company on that cap. You are essentially drawing a line in the sand (albeit a small one and in some cases it doesn't actually affect the ultimate valuation) of what your company is worth in the future.

From the entrepreneur's standpoint, the choice isn't clear, either. Some argue that the convertible debt structure, by definition, leads to a higher ultimate price for the first round. We won't go as far as to say they are right, but we can see the argument that with a convertible debt feature you are allowing an inflated price based on time to positively impact the valuation for the past investors. We'd argue that this is missing half of the analysis in that a founder's first investors are sometimes the most important. These are the people who invested in you at the riskiest stage before anyone else would. You like them, you respect them, and you might even be related to them. Assume that you create a lot of value along the way and the equity investor prices the round at a number that is higher than even you expected. Your first investors will own less than anyone anticipated. At the end of the day, your biggest fans are happy about the financing, but sad that they own so little.

But does it really set a higher price? Let's go back to the example of a convertible debt round with a cap. If we were going to agree to this deal, our cap would be the price that we would have agreed to in an equity round. So, in effect, you've just sold the same amount of equity to us, but we have an option for the price to be lower than we would have offered you since there are plenty of scenarios in which the equity price is below the cap amount. Why on earth would I agree to a cap that is above the price that I'm willing to pay today? The cap amounts to a ceiling on your price. VCs will focus on that cap as well. There are plenty of situations where the VCs would have been willing to pay $X per share, but after seeing the cap number in due diligence prior to a term sheet they offer only $Y (less than $X) per share because it's within the cap. So while you may have gotten a better deal on your seed round, your Series A round (which normally sees the company raising a lot more money than a seed round) is now underpriced compared to what it could be. In the aggregate, the company actually underpriced itself in this scenario.

The Entrepreneur's Perspective

To attract seed stage investors, consider a convertible debt deal with two additional features: a reasonable time horizon on an equity financing and a forced conversion if that horizon isn't met, as well as a floor, not a ceiling, on the conversion valuation.

There's also some dissonance here since VCs spend a lot of their time valuing companies and negotiating on price. If your VC can't or won't do this, what is this telling you? Do you and the VC have radically different views of the value proposition you've created? Will this impact the relationship going forward or the way that each of you strategically thinks about your company?

The Discount

Remember that a convertible debt deal doesn't purchase equity in your company. Instead, it's simply a loan that has the ability to convert to equity based on some future financing event. Let's begin our discussion of terms for convertible debt with the most important one, the *discount*.

Until recently, we had never seen a convertible debt deal that didn't convert at a discount to the next financing round. Given some of the current excited market conditions at the seed stage, we've heard of convertible deals with no discount, but view this as irregular and not sustainable over the long term.

The idea behind the discount is that investors should get, or require, more upside than just the interest rate associated with the debt for the risk that they are taking by investing early. These investors aren't banks—they are planning to own equity in the company, but are simply deferring the price discussion to the next financing.

So how does the discount work? There are two approaches: the discounted price to the next round and warrants. We'll cover the discounted price approach in this section, as it's much simpler and better oriented for a seed round investment.

For the discounted price to the next round, you might see something like this in the legal documents:

> This Note shall automatically convert in whole without any further action by the Holders into such Equity Securities at a

conversion price equal to eighty percent (80%) of the price per
share paid by the Investors purchasing the Equity Securities on
the same terms and conditions as given to the Investors.

This means that if your next round investors are paying $1.00 per
share, then the note will convert into the same shares at a 20 percent
discount, or $0.80 per share. For example, if you have a $100,000
convertible note, it will purchase 125,000 shares ($100,000/$0.80)
whereas the new equity investor will get 100,000 shares for his investment of $100,000 ($100,000/$1.00).

The range of discounts we typically see is 10 to 30 percent, with
20 percent being the most common. While occasionally you'll see a
discount that increases over time (e.g., 10 percent if the round closes
in 90 days, 20 percent if it takes longer), we generally recommend
entrepreneurs (and investors) keep this simple—it is the seed round,
after all.

Valuation Caps

The next economic term is the *valuation cap*, also known as the cap.
The cap is an investor-favorable term that puts a ceiling on the conversion price of the debt. The valuation cap is typically seen only in
seed rounds where the investors are concerned that the next round
of financing will be at a price that is at a valuation that wouldn't reward them appropriately for taking a risk by investing early in the
seed round.

For example, an investor wants to invest $100,000 in a company
and thinks that the premoney valuation of the company is somewhere in the $2 million to $4 million range. The entrepreneur thinks
the valuation should be higher. Either way, the investor and the entrepreneur agree to not deal with a valuation negotiation and instead
decide to consummate a convertible debt deal with a 20 percent discount to the next round.

Nine months pass and the company is doing well. The entrepreneur is happy and the investor is happy. The company goes to
raise a round of financing in the form of preferred stock. It receives a
term sheet at a $20 million premoney valuation. In this case, the dis-
count of 20 percent would result in the investor having an effective
valuation of $16 million for his investment nine months ago.

On one hand the investor is happy for the entrepreneur but on
the other hand he is shocked by the relatively high valuation for his

investment. He realizes he made a bad decision by not pricing the deal initially, as anything below $16 million would have been better for him. Of course, this is nowhere near the $2 million to $4 million the investor was contemplating the company was worth at the time he made the convertible debt investment.

The valuation cap addresses this situation. By agreeing on a cap, the entrepreneur and the investor can still defer the price discussion, but set a ceiling at which point the conversion price caps.

In our previous example, let's assume that the entrepreneur and the investor agree on a $4 million cap. Since the deal has a 20 percent discount, any valuation up to $5 million will result in the investor getting a discount of 20 percent. Once the discounted value goes above the cap, then the cap will apply. So, in the case of the $20 million premoney valuation, the investor will get shares at an effective price of $4 million.

As we've mentioned, in some cases, caps can impact the valuation of the next round. Some VCs will look at the cap and view it as a price ceiling to the next round price, assuming that it was the high point negotiated between the seed investors and the entrepreneur. To mitigate this, entrepreneurs should try to not disclose the seed round terms until a price has been agreed to with a new VC investor. Lately we've been seeing a lot of VCs ask for the terms of the convertible debt round before they are willing to issue a term sheet. We understand that it is hard for an entrepreneur to say no to a potential funding partner's requests.

Clearly, entrepreneurs would prefer not to have valuation caps. However, many seed investors recognize that an uncapped note has the potential to create a big risk/return disparity, especially in frothy markets for early stage deals. We believe that—over the long term—caps create more alignment between entrepreneurs and seed investors as long as the price cap is thoughtfully negotiated based on the stage of the company.

Interest Rate

Since convertible debt is a loan, it almost always has an *interest rate* associated with it, as that's the minimum upside an investor is going to want to have for the investment.

We believe interest rates on convertible debt should be as low as possible. This isn't bank debt, and the funders are being fairly compensated through the use of whatever type of discount has been negotiated. If you are an entrepreneur, check out what the applicable federal rates (AFRs) are to see the lowest legally allowable interest rates; bump them up just a little bit (for volatility), and suggest whatever that number is.

Realizing that the discount and the interest rate are often linked, we'll usually see an interest rate between 6 percent and 12 percent associated with a discount between 10 percent and 30 percent.

Conversion Mechanics

Eventually the convertible debt will convert into equity. There are several nuances around how and when the note will convert. These *conversion mechanics* are important but can usually be configured in a way where everyone will be happy with them if they concentrate on defining them up front.

In general, debt holders have traditionally enjoyed superior control rights over companies and the ability to force nasty things like bankruptcy and involuntary liquidations. Therefore, having outstanding debt (that doesn't convert) can be a bad thing if an entrepreneur ever gets sideways with one of the debt holders. While it's not talked about that much, it happens often, and we've seen it many times leave the debt holder in a great position of leverage in negotiations.

Here is typical conversion language:

> In the event that Payor issues and sells shares of its Equity Securities to investors (the "Investors") on or before [180] days from the date herewith (the "Maturity Date") in an equity financing with total proceeds to the Payor of not less than $1,000,000 (excluding the conversion of the Notes or other debt) (a "Qualified Financing"), then the outstanding principal balance of this Note shall automatically convert in whole without any further action by the Holders into such Equity Securities at a conversion price equal to the price per share paid by the Investors purchasing the Equity Securities on the same terms and conditions as given to the Investors.

Let's take a look at what matters in this paragraph. Notice that in order for the note to convert automatically, all of the conditions must be met. If not, there is no automatic conversion.

- *Term.* Here, the company must sell equity within six months (180 days) for the debt to automatically convert. Consider whether this is enough time. If we were entrepreneurs, we'd try to get this period to be as long as possible. Many venture firms are not allowed (by their agreements with their investors) to issue debt that has a maturity date longer than a year, so don't be surprised if one year is the maximum that you can negotiate if you are dealing with a VC investor.
- *Amount.* In this case the company must raise $1,000,000 of new money, (because the conversion of the outstanding debt is excluded) for the debt to convert. The entrepreneur often gets to decide the amount (based on the minimum the company is hoping to raise). When you determine this number, think about how long you have (here 180 days) and how much you think you can reasonably raise in that time period.

So what happens if the company does not achieve the milestones to automatically convert the debt? The debt stays outstanding unless the debt holders agree to convert their holdings. This is when voting control comes into play. It is important to pay attention to the amendment provision in the notes.

> Any term of this Note may be amended or waived with the written consent of Payor and the Majority Holders. Upon the effectuation of such waiver or amendment in conformance with this Section 11, the Payor shall promptly give written notice thereof to the record Holders of the Notes who have not previously consented thereto in writing.

While one will never see anything less than a majority of holders needing to consent to an amendment (and thus a different standard for conversion), make sure the standard doesn't get too high. For instance, if you had two parties splitting $1,000,000 in convertible debt with a 60/40 percentage split, you only need one party to consent if the majority rules, but both parties would need to consent if a supermajority must approve. Little things like this can make a big difference if the 40 percent holder is the one you aren't getting along with at the present moment.

Conversion in a Sale of the Company

What happens to the convertible debt if the company gets acquired before there is an equity financing and before the debt is converted to equity? There are a few different scenarios.

The lender gets its money back plus interest. If there is no specific language addressing this situation, this is what usually ends up happening. In this case, the convertible debt document doesn't allow the debt to convert into anything, but at the same time mandates that upon a sale the debt must be paid off. So the lenders don't see any of the upside on the acquisition. The potentially bad news is that if the merger is an all-stock deal, the company will need to find a way to find cash to pay back the loan or negotiate a way for the acquiring company to deal with the debt.

The lender gets its money back, plus interest plus a multiple of the original principal amount. In this case, the documents dictate that the company will pay back outstanding principal plus interest and then a multiple on the original investment. Usually we see a multiple of two to three times, but in later stage companies this multiple can be even higher. Typical language follows.

> Sale of the Company: If a Qualified Financing has not occurred and the Company elects to consummate a sale of the Company prior to the Maturity Date, then notwithstanding any provision of the Notes to the contrary (i) the Company will give the Investors at least five days prior written notice of the anticipated closing date of such sale of the Company and (ii) the Company will pay the holder of each Note an aggregate amount equal to _____ times the aggregate amount of principal and interest then outstanding under such Note in full satisfaction of the Company's obligations under such Note.

Some sort of conversion does occur. In the case of an early stage company that hasn't issued preferred stock yet, the debt converts into stock of the acquiring company (if it's a stock deal) at a valuation subject to a cap. If it's not a stock deal, then one normally sees one of the preceding scenarios.

With later stage companies, the investors usually structure the convertible notes to have the most flexibility. They either get a multiple payout on the debt or get the equity upside based on the previous preferred round price. Note that if the acquisition price is low, the holders of the debt may usually opt out of conversion and demand cash payment on the notes.

While in many cases issuing convertible debt is easier to deal with than issuing equity, the one situation where this often becomes complex is an acquisition while the debt is outstanding. Our strong advice is to address in the documents how the debt will be handled in an acquisition.

Warrants

A few sections ago we discussed the "discounted price to the next round" approach to providing a discount on convertible debt. The other approach to a discount is to issue *warrants*. This approach is more complex and usually applies only to situations where the company has already raised a round of equity, but it occasionally pops up in early stage deals. If you are doing a seed round, we encourage you not to use this approach and instead to save some legal fees. However, if you are doing a later stage convertible debt round or your investors insist on you issuing warrants, here's how it works.

Assume that once again the investor is investing $100,000 and receives warrant coverage in the amount of 20 percent of the amount of the convertible note. In this case the investor will get a warrant for $20,000.

This is where it can get a little tricky. What does $20,000 worth of warrants mean? A warrant is an option to purchase a certain number of shares at a predetermined price. But how do you figure out the number of warrants and the price that the warrants will be at? There are numerous different ways to calculate this, such as:

- $20,000 worth of common stock at the last value ascribed to either the common or the preferred stock.
- $20,000 worth of the last round of preferred stock at that round's price of the stock.
- $20,000 worth of the next round of preferred stock at whatever price that happens to be.

As you can see, the actual percentage of the company associated with the warrants can vary greatly depending on the price of the security that underlies it. As a bonus, the particular ownership of certain classes may affect voting control of a particular class of stock.

If there is a standard, it's the second version where the warrants are attached to the prior preferred stock round. If there is no prior preferred, then one normally sees the stock convert to the next preferred round unless an acquisition of the company occurs before a preferred round is consummated; in that case, it reverts to the common stock.

For example, assume that the round gets done at $1.00 per share, just like in the previous example. The investor who holds a $100,000 convertible note will get $20,000 of warrants, or 20,000 warrants at an exercise price of $1.00, to go along with the 100,000 shares received in the financing from the conversion of the note.

Warrants have a few extra terms that matter.

- *Term length.* The length of time the warrants are exercisable, which is typically five to 10 years. Shorter is better for the entrepreneur and company. Longer is better for the investor.
- *Merger considerations.* What happens to the warrants in the event the company is acquired? We can't opine more strongly that all warrants should expire at a merger unless they are exercised just prior to the transaction. In other words, the warrant holder must decide to either exercise or give up the warrants if the company is acquired. Acquiring companies hate buying companies that have warrants that survive a merger and allow the warrant holder to buy equity in the acquirer. Many mergers have been held up because warrants with this feature have upset the potential acquirer and thus as part of the closing requirements the acquirer has mandated that the company go out and repurchase or edit the terms of the warrants. This is not a good negotiating spot for the company to find itself in, as it will have to pay off warrant holders while disclosing the potential merger (so the company will have little leverage) and at the same time will have a sword hanging over its head by the acquirer until the issue is resolved.
- *Original issue discount (OID).* This is an accounting issue that is boring, yet important. If a convertible debt deal includes warrants, the warrants must be paid for separately in order to avoid the OID issue. In other words, if the debt is for $100,000 and there is 20 percent warrant coverage, the IRS says that

the warrants themselves have some value. If there is no provision for the actual purchase of the warrants, the lender will have received an original issue discount, which says that the $100,000 debt was issued at a discount since the lender also received warrants. The problem is that part of the $100,000 principal repaid will be included as interest to the lender or, even worse, it will be accrued as income over the life of the note even before any payments are made. The easy fix is to pay something for the warrants, which usually is an amount in the low thousands of dollars.

The difference between warrants and discounts is probably insignificant for the investor. We suppose if the investor is able to get warrants for common stock, then perhaps the ultimate value of warrants may outweigh the discount, but it's not clear. As evidenced by the number of words we have devoted to the topic, warrants add a fair amount of complexity and legal costs to the mix. However, some discounts will include valuation caps, and that can create some negative company valuation ramifications. Warrants completely stay away from the valuation discussion.

Finally, in no case should an entrepreneur let an investor double-dip and receive both a discount and warrants. That's not a reasonable position for investors to take—they should either get a discount or get warrants.

Other Terms

There are a few other terms that sometimes show up in a convertible debt deal. You'll recognize these from the earlier chapters on terms in an equity financing, as they are the terms that more sophisticated angels or seed investors will insist on to preserve their rights in later financings.

The first term you'll occasionally see in a convertible debt financing in a *pro rata right*, which will allow debt holders to participate proratably in a future financing. Since many times the dollar amounts are relatively low in a convertible debt deal, investors may ask for super pro rata rights. For instance, if an investor invests $500,000 in a convertible debt deal and the company later raises $7,000,000, the investor's pro rata investment rights wouldn't allow the investor to purchase a large portion of the next round. As a result, the seed investor may ask for a pro rata right for two to four times the investor's current ownership or for a specific percentage (say 5 percent to 20 percent) of the next financing. While pro rata rights are pretty typical, if you have people asking for super pro rata rights or a specific portion of the next financing, you should be careful, as granting these will limit your long-term financing options.

Every now and then you'll see a *liquidation preference* in a convertible debt deal. It works the same way as in a preferred stock deal: the investors get their money back first, or a multiple of their money back first, before any proceeds are distributed to anyone else. This usually happens in the case when a company is struggling to raise capital and current investors offer a convertible debt (also called a bridge loan) deal to the company. Back in the good old days, usury laws prevented such terms; but in most states this is not an issue and the investors are allowed to have not only the security of holding debt, but the upside of preferred stock should a liquidation event occur.

Early Stage versus Late Stage Dynamics

Traditionally, convertible debt was issued by mid to late stage startups that needed a financing to get them to a place where they believed they could raise more money. Thus, these deals were called bridge financings.

The terms were basically the same unless the company was faring poorly and there was doubt about the ability to raise new capital, or the bridge was to get the company to an acquisition or an orderly shutdown. In these cases, one saw terms like liquidation preferences and in some cases changes to board or voting control come into play. Some of these bridge loans also contained terms like pay-to-play that we discussed earlier in Chapter 4.

Given the traditional complexity and cost of legal fees associated with preferred stock financings, however, convertible debt became a common way to make seed stage investments, as it tended to be simpler and less expensive from a legal perspective. Over time, equity rounds have become cheaper to consummate, and the legal fees argument doesn't carry much weight these days. In the end, the main force driving the use of convertible debt in early stage companies is the parties' desire to avoid setting a valuation.

Can Convertible Debt Be Dangerous?

One final issue with convertible debt is a technical legal one. You'll have to forgive us, but Jason is an ex-lawyer and sometimes we can't keep him in his cage.

If a company raises cash via equity, it has a positive balance sheet. It is solvent (assets are greater than obligations), and the board and executives have fiduciary duties to the shareholders in the efforts to maximize company value. The shareholders are all the usual suspects: the employees and VCs. Life is good and normal.

However, if a company is insolvent, the board and company may (based in large part on state law—ask your attorney) now owe fiduciary duties to the creditors of the company. By definition, if you raise a convertible debt round, your company is insolvent. You have cash, but your debt obligations are greater than your assets. Your creditors include your landlord, anyone you owe money to (including former disgruntled employees), and founders who have lawyers.

How does this change the paradigm? To be fair, we have had no personal war stories here, but it's not hard to construct some weird situations.

Let's look at the hypothetical situation.

Assume the company is not a success and fails. In the case of raising equity, the officers and directors owe a duty only to the creditors (e.g., the landlord) at such time that cash isn't large enough to pay their liabilities. If the company manages it correctly, creditors are paid off cleanly even on the downside scenario. But sometimes it doesn't happen this way and there are lawsuits. When the lawyers get involved, they'll look to establish the time in which the company went insolvent and then try to show that the actions of the board were bad during that time. If the time frame is short, it's hard to make a case against the company.

However, if you raise debt, the insolvency time lasts until your debt converts into equity. As a result, if your company ends up failing and you can't pay your creditors, the ability for a plaintiff lawyer to judge your actions has increased dramatically. And don't forget: if you have any outstanding employment litigation, all of these folks count as creditors as well.

The worst part of this is that many states impose personal liability on directors for things that occur while a company is insolvent. This means that some states will allow creditors to sue directors personally for not getting all of the money they are owed.

Now, we don't want to get too crazy here. We are talking about early stage and seed companies, and hopefully the situation is clean enough that these doomsday predictions won't happen; but our bet is that few folks participating in convertible debt rounds are actually thinking about these issues. While we don't know of any actual cases out there, we've been around this business long enough to know that there is constant innovation in the plaintiff's bar as well.

CHAPTER 9

How Venture Capital Funds Work

Before we talk about the dynamics of the negotiation of the deal, it's useful to understand the motivation of the person you'll be negotiating against, namely the venture capitalist (VC). We've been asked many times to divulge the deep, dark secrets of what makes VCs tick. One night over dinner we talked through much of this with a very experienced entrepreneur who was in the middle of a negotiation for a late stage round for his company. At the end of the discussion, he implored us to put pen to paper since even though he was extremely experienced and had been involved in several VC-backed companies, our conversation helped him understand the nuances of what he was dealing with, which, until our explanation, had been confusing him.

In general, it's important to understand what drives your current and future business partners, namely your VCs, as their motivations will impact your business. While the basics of how a venture fund works may be known, in this chapter we try to also cover all the nonobvious issues that play into how VCs think and behave. To do that, we'll dive into how funds are set up and managed as well as the pressures (both internally and externally) that VCs face.

Overview of a Typical Structure

Let's start by describing a typical *VC fund* structure (see illustration). There are three basic entities that make up the fund. The first entity is the *management company* and is usually owned by the senior partners. The management company employs all of the people with whom you interact at the firm, such as the partners, associates, and support staff, and pays for all of the normal day-to-day business expenses such as the firm's office lease and monthly Internet expense.

As a result, the management company is essentially the franchise of the firm. While old funds are retired and new funds are raised, the management company lives on and services each of the funds that are raised. A VC's business card almost always lists the name of the management company, which is one of the reasons that the signature blocks on a term sheet often have a different name than the one you are used to associating with the firm. For example, in our case, Foundry Group is the name of our management company, not that of the actual funds that we raise and invest from.

The next entity is the *limited partnership* (LP) vehicle. When a VC talks about his "fund" or that his firm "raised a fund of $225 million," he is actually talking about a limited partnership vehicle that contains the investors in the fund (also called limited partners, or LPs).

The final entity is one an entrepreneur rarely hears of called the *general partnership* (GP) entity. This is the legal entity for serving as the actual general partner to the fund. In some partnerships, the individual managing directors play this role, but over time this has evolved into a separate legal entity that the managing directors each own on a fund-by-fund basis.

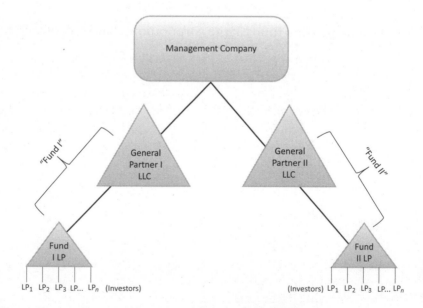

Management Company Structure: General Partnership and Limited Partnership

We realize this is confusing unless you are in law school, in which case you are likely salivating with joy over the legal complexity we are exposing you to. The key point to remember is that there is separation between the management company (the franchise) and the actual funds that it raises (the LP entities). These distinct entities will often have divergent interests and motivations, especially as managing directors join or leave the VC firm. One managing director may be your point of contact today, but this person may have different alignments among his multiple organizations that will potentially affect you.

How Firms Raise Money

The next time you are on the fund-raising trail beating your head against the wall trying to get through to a VC about how awesome your business is, remember that VCs also get to enjoy the same process when raising funds. So, while we feel your pain, we also admit that many VCs quickly forget about the whole process and inflict too much pain on the entrepreneurs raising money. While this knowledge might help a little when you are sitting frustrated in your hotel room after another day of fund-raising, we encourage you to also discover the magic soothing properties of Scotch.

VCs raise money from a variety of entities, including government and corporate pension funds, large corporations, banks, professional institutional investors, educational endowments, high-net-worth individuals, funds of funds, charitable organizations, and insurance companies. The arrangement between the VCs and their investors is subject to a long, complicated contract known as the *limited partnership agreement* (LPA) that makes one thing clear: VCs have bosses also—their investors, also known as their LPs.

When a VC firm makes an announcement that it has raised a $100 million fund, it is not the case that the VC has $100 million sitting in the bank waiting for a smart entrepreneur to come along. The VC firm normally keeps very little cash on hand and must ask its LPs every time it wants money to make an investment. This is known as a *capital call*, and it typically takes two weeks from the moment the money is requested until it arrives. Note that the LPs are legally obligated under the fund agreements to send the VCs money every time they make a capital call.

If a VC firm requests money and its investors say no, things get tricky. The VC usually has some very draconian rights in the LPA to enforce its capital call, but we've seen several moments in history when VCs have done a capital call and there has been a smaller amount of money to be had than anticipated. This is not a good thing if you are the entrepreneur relying on getting a deal done with the VC. Fortunately, this is a rare occurrence.

Why might investors refuse to fund a capital call? For one, LPs may think the VC is making bad decisions and may want to get out of the fund. More likely, something exogenous has happened to the LPs and they are feeling tight on cash and can't, or don't want to, comply with the capital call. This happened a number of times in the global economic crisis in the fall of 2008 (and even back in 2001) when three categories of LPs were impacted:

1. High-net-worth individuals who were feeling lower-net-worth at the time.
2. Banks that had no cash available (and quickly became parts of other banks).
3. Endowments, foundations, and charitable organizations that had massive cash flow crises because of their ratio of illiquid investments.

In many cases, the VC will find a new LP to buy the old LP's interest. There is an active market known as a secondary market for LPs who want to sell their interest. Economically, this is almost always more attractive to the LP than not making a capital call, so except in moments of extreme stress, the VC usually ends up with the money to make an investment.

How Venture Capitalists Make Money

Now that we've explained the structure of a typical VC fund, let's explore how VCs get paid. The compensation dynamics of a particular fund often impact the behavior of a VC early in the life of a company, as well as later on when the company is either succeeding or struggling and needs to raise additional capital.

Management Fees

VCs' salaries come from their funds' *management fees*. The management fee is a percentage (typically between 1.5 percent and 2.5 percent) of the total amount of money committed to a fund. These fees are taken annually (paid out quarterly or semi-annually) and finance the operations of the VC firm, including all of the salaries for the investing partners and their staff. For example, if a VC firm raises a $100 million fund with a 2 percent management fee, each year the firm will receive $2 million in management fees. While this may seem like a lot of money, it goes to pay all of the costs of the VC firm, including employees, partners, associates, rent, flying around the country seeing entrepreneurs, copiers, diet soda, and brand-new MacBook Airs.

The percentage is usually inversely related to the size of fund; the smaller the fund, the larger the percentage—but most funds level out around 2 percent. There's a slight nuance, which is the fee paid during and after the *commitment period*, or the period of time when the fund can make new investments—usually the first five years. This fee, which is usually 2 to 2.5 percent, begins to decrease after the end of the commitment period. The formula varies widely, but in most firms the average total fee over a 10-year period is about 15 percent of the committed capital. So, in our previous $100 million fund example, the typical fund will have $15 million of management fees to run its operations and pay its people.

But wait, there's more. Most VC firms raise multiple funds. The average firm raises a new fund every three or four years, but some firms raise funds more frequently while others have multiple different fund vehicles such as an early stage fund, a growth stage fund, and a China fund. In these cases, the fees stack up across funds. If a firm raises a fund every three years, it has a new management fee that adds to its old management fee. The simple way to think of this is that the management fee is roughly 2 percent of total committed capital across all funds. So, if Fund 1 is a $100 million fund and Fund 2 is a $200 million fund, the management fee ends up being approximately $6 million annually ($2 million for Fund 1 and $4 million for Fund 2).

Although VC firms tend to grow head count (partners and staff) as they raise new funds, this isn't always the case and the head count rarely grows in direct proportion to the increased management fees. As a result, the senior partners of the VC firm (or the ones with a managing director title) see their base compensation rise with each additional fund. The dynamics vary widely from firm to firm, but you can assume that as the capital under management increases, so do the fees and, as a result, the salaries of some of the managing directors.

The VC firm gets this management fee completely independently of its investing success. Over the long term, the only consequence of investment success on the fee is the ability of the firm to raise additional funds. If the firm does not generate meaningful positive returns, over time it will have difficulty raising additional funds. However, this isn't an overnight phenomenon, as the fee arrangements for each fund are guaranteed for 10 years. We've been known to say that "it takes a decade to kill a venture capital firm," and the extended fee dynamic is a key part of this.

Carried Interest

Even though the management fees can be substantial, in a success case the real money that a VC makes, known as the *carried interest*, or *carry*, should dwarf the management fee. Carry is the profit that VCs get after returning money to their investors (the LPs). If we use our $100 million fund example, VCs receive their carry after they've returned $100 million to their LPs. Most VCs get 20 percent of the profits after returning capital (a 20 percent carry), although some long-standing or extremely successful funds take up to 30 percent of the profits.

Let's play out our example. Again, start with the $100 million fund. Assume that it's a successful fund and returns 3× the capital, or $300 million. In this case, the first $100 million goes back to the LPs, and the remaining profit, or $200 million, is split 80 percent to the LPs and 20 percent to the GPs. The VC firm gets $40 million in carried interest and the LPs get the remaining $160 million. And yes, in this case everyone is very happy.

Remember that this firm received about $15 million of management fees over a decade for this fund. However, there's an interesting nuance here. If the fund is a $100 million fund and $15 million goes to management fees, doesn't that leave only $85 million to invest? In some cases it does, but VCs are allowed to recycle their management fee and subsequently reinvest it up to the total of $100 million. This assumes returns early enough in the life of the fund to recycle and in some cases careful cash flow management, but all firms should be motivated to get the entire $100 million to work. In this case, the $15 million management fee can actually be viewed as a prepayment on carry since it is essentially getting reinvested from proceeds from the fund. All LPs should favor recycling, as their goal is generally cash-on-cash return. Getting more money to work, namely the full $100 million instead of only $85 million, enhances the total return.

Note that we have been talking about the VC firm as a whole, not any individual managing director or other investment professional in the firm. An individual VC could quadruple the amount of money invested in his particular companies, but still receive no carry on a fund due to poor investment decisions made by the other partners. In addition, most firms do not have equal allocation of carry between partners, with the senior partners tending to get disproportionately more than the younger partners. Over time this can be a major source of friction within the firm if either there is inequitable behavior from the senior partners or other firms offer the young star performers better economic incentives and pick them off. This gets especially difficult when a fund, or a series of funds, is performing poorly yet the positive returns are coming from one or two partners.

Those of you sophisticated in the art of fund structure will note that we've neglected to point out that LPs want their VCs to invest in their own fund. Historically there has been a 99 percent/1 percent split between the LPs and the GPs, where the VC partners put in their own money alongside the LPs for 1 percent of the fund (e.g., in our $100 million fund example, the LPs would put in $99 million and the GPs would put in $1 million). The *GP commitment* historically was 1 percent but has floated up over time and is occasionally as high as 5 percent.

While carry sounds like a wonderful thing, there is one risky situation around it called the *clawback*. Again, assume our $100 million fund. Let's also assume the VCs have called only half of the fund ($50 million). If the $50 million invested so far returns $80 million, the fund is in a profit situation where $50 million has been returned and there is $30 million in profit that the VCs have the right to take their carry on. The VCs happily pocket their $6 million, assuming the carry is 20 percent. But what happens if the VCs call and invest the rest of the fund and it's a bust, returning a total of only $100 million? At the end of the fund, the VCs would have invested $100 million, but returned only $100 million, and as a result should get no carry.

So what happens to the $6 million they took in the middle of the fund life? The $6 million is clawed back from the VCs and given back to the LPs. While logical in theory, it's harder in practice. Assume the VC fund has four equal partners who have each received a

$1.5 million carry check. These were happy days, followed by some not so happy days when the fund performed poorly. Along the way, two of the VCs left the firm to go to other firms, and the remaining two partners no longer talk to them. In fact, one of the remaining partners got divorced and gave half of his money to his ex-spouse. And one of the other VCs declared bankruptcy after overextending himself financially. Oh, and all four of them have paid taxes on their carry.

The LPs don't care. They want the $6 million that is owed to them, and many fund agreements state that each partner is liable for the full amount, regardless of what they actually received in profit distributions. So, it's possible that a subset of the partnership has to pay back the LPs and fight with the current and former partners for the rest. It's not pretty and we wish this were only a hypothetical situation, but it's not.

Reimbursement for Expenses

There is one other small income stream that VCs receive: reimbursements from the companies they invest in for expenses associated with board meetings. VCs will charge all reasonable expenses associated with board meetings to the company they are visiting. This usually isn't a big deal unless your VC always flies on his private plane and stays at the presidential suite at your local Four Seasons hotel. In the case where you feel your VC is spending excessively and charging everything back to the company, you should feel comfortable confronting the VC. If you aren't, enlist one of your more frugal board members to help.

How Time Impacts Fund Activity

VC fund agreements have two concepts that govern the ability to invest over time. The first concept is called the commitment period. The commitment period (also called "investment period"), which is usually five years, is the length of time that a VC has for identifying and investing in new companies in the fund. Once the commitment period is over, the fund can no longer invest in new companies, but it can invest additional money in existing portfolio companies. This is one of the main reasons that VC firms typically raise a new fund every three to five years—once they've committed to all the companies they are going to invest in from a fund, they need to raise a new fund to stay active as investors in new companies.

It's sad but true that some VCs who are past their commitment period and have not raised a new fund still meet with entrepreneurs trying to raise money. In these cases, the entrepreneur has no idea that there is no chance the VCs will invest, but the VCs get to pretend they are still actively investing and try to maintain some semblance of deal flow even though they can't invest any longer. We first saw this in 2006 and 2007 as firms that raised their previous fund in 2000 or 2001 struggled to raise a new fund. Over time the media picked up on this dynamic and started referring to these firms as the "walking dead"—zombie-like VCs who were still acting like VCs, earning management fees from their old funds and actively managing their old portfolios, but not making new investments.

The good zombies are open about their status; the not so good ones keep taking meetings with new companies even though they can't make new investments. It's usually easy to spot zombie VCs—just ask them when they made their last new investment. If it's more than a year ago, it's likely they are a zombie. You can also ask simple questions like "How many new investments will you make out of your current fund?" or "When do you expect to be raising a new fund?" If you feel like the VCs are giving you ambiguous answers, they are probably a zombie.

The other concept is called the *investment term*, or the length of time that the fund can remain active. New investments can be made only during the commitment/investment period, but follow-on investments can be made during the investment term. A typical VC fund has a 10-year investment term with two one-year options to extend, although some have three one-year extensions or one two-year extension. Twelve years may sound like plenty of time, but when an early stage fund makes a new seed investment in its fifth year and the time frame for exit for an average investment can stretch out over a decade, 12 years is often a constraint. As a result, many early stage funds go on for longer than 12 years—occasionally up to as many as 17 years.

Once you get past 12 years, the LPs have to affirmatively vote every year to have the GP continue to operate the fund. In cases in which a firm has continued to raise additional funds, the LPs are generally supportive of this continued fund extension activity. There is often a negotiation over the management fee being charged to continue to manage the fund, with it ranging from a lower percentage of remaining invested capital (say, 1 percent) all the way to waiving the fee entirely. This isn't an issue for a firm that has raised additional funds and has the management fee from those funds to cover its operations, but it is a major issue for zombie firms that find their annual operating fees materially declining. Time is not the friend of a zombie firm, as partners begin to leave for greener pastures, spend less and less time helping the companies they've invested in, or simply start pushing the companies to sell and generate liquidity.

In some cases, entire portfolios are sold to new firms via what is called a *secondary sale* in which someone else takes over managing the portfolio through the liquidation of the companies. In these cases, the people the entrepreneurs are dealing with, including their board members, can change completely. These secondary buyers often have a very different agenda than the original investor, usually much more focused on driving the company to a speedy exit, even at a lower value than the other LPs.

The Entrepreneur's Perspective

One important thing to understand about your prospective investor's fund is how old the fund is. The closer the fund is to its end of life, the more problematic things can become for you in terms of investor pressure for liquidity (in which your interests and the investor's might not be aligned), or an investor requirement to distribute shares in your company to LPs, which could be horrible for you if the firm has a large number of LPs who then become direct shareholders.

Reserves

Reserves are the amount of investment capital that is allocated to each company that a VC invests in. This is a very important concept that most entrepreneurs don't pay proper attention to. Imagine that a VC invests $1 million in the first round of your company. At the time of making the investment, the VC will reserve a theoretical future amount of the fund to invest in follow-on rounds. The VC generally won't tell you this amount, but it's usually a well-defined amount within the VC firm.

Typically, but not always, the earlier the stage a company is at, the more reserves the VC will allocate. In the case of a late stage investment immediately prior to an IPO, a VC might not have any reserves allocated to a company, whereas a first-round investment might have reserves of $10 million or more associated with it.

While most VCs will ask the entrepreneur about future funding needs prior to making an investment, many VCs ignore this number and come up with their own view of the future financing dynamics and the corresponding reserves amount. In our experience, entrepreneurs are often optimistic about how much capital they need, estimating on the low side. VCs will rely on their own experience when figuring out reserves and will often be conservative and estimate high early in the life of the investment, reducing this number over time as a company ages.

Let's look at how reserve analysis can impact a company. Assume a VC firm has a $100 million fund and invests a total of $50 million into 10 different companies. Assume also that the VC firm has an aggregate of $50 million in reserves divided between the 10 companies. While it doesn't matter if the firm is accurately reserved on a company by company basis at the beginning, the total amount reserved and how it is deployed over time are critical. If the VC has underreserved and $70 million ends up being needed in aggregate to support the ongoing funding of the 10 companies, the VC firm won't have the ability to continue to fund all of the companies it is an investor in. This usually results in VCs picking favorites and not supporting some of the companies. Although this can manifest itself as VCs simply walking away from their investments or being direct that they have no additional money to invest, the behavior by the VC is usually more mysterious. The less upfront VC will often actively resist additional financings, try to limit the size and subsequently the dilution of these financings, or push you to sell the company. In cases where a pay-to-play term is in effect, you'll often see more resistance to additional financings as the VC firm tries to protect its position in the company, even if it's not necessarily the right thing to do for the business.

Overreserving, or reserving $50 million when you ultimately need only $30 million, is also an issue, but it doesn't impact the entrepreneurs. Overreserving results in the VC underinvesting the fund, which is economically disadvantageous to the LPs and the VCs. The LPs want all of the fund capital to be invested because it increases the chance of returning more capital. The VCs also want to get all the money to work, especially when funds become profitable, as the greater the absolute return, the greater the carry.

Most VC fund agreements allow a firm to raise a new fund once they are around 70 percent committed and reserved. While this threshold varies by firms, it is usually reasonably high. As a result, there is a slight motivation to overreserve to reach this threshold that is countered by the negative economic dynamics of not fully investing the fund. Of course, independent of the threshold, the VC still needs to have good performance and the support of the existing investors to raise a new fund.

The Entrepreneur's Perspective

You should understand how much capital the firm reserves for follow-on investments per company, or in the case of your company in particular. If you think your company is likely to need multiple rounds of financing, you want to make sure the VC has plenty of "dry powder" in reserve for your company so you don't end up in contentious situations down the road in which your investor has no more money left to invest and is then at odds with you or with future investors.

Cash Flow

VCs have to pay as much attention to cash flow as entrepreneurs do, although many don't until they run into trouble. Remember that the capital raised by a venture firm can be used for investments in companies, management fees, and expenses of the fund, which include paying accountants for an annual audit and tax filings and paying lawyers for any litigation issues. Also remember that LPs want their VCs to invest 100 percent of the fund in companies.

If a VC has a $100 million fund with a typical management fee, approximately $15 million will be spent on noninvesting activity during the life of the fund. This means to fully invest the $100 million, the fund will need to generate $15 million of returns that it can recycle—or invest—over the life of the fund. More important is that timing matters since the exits that generate this additional cash are unpredictable, and as a fund gets later in its life, it can start to get into a position where it doesn't actually have the cash to recycle.

In the most extreme case, the firm will underreserve and not manage cash flow effectively. As a result, it will find itself crunched at both ends. It won't have adequate reserves to continue to support its investments and, even if it did, it won't have the cash to pay its employees through management fees. This situation can occur even in firms that have raised follow-on funds, as the cash flow dynamics of recycling are fund specific.

Cross-Fund Investing

Many VC firms invest out of several linked fund entities (e.g., you may have two funds as investors in your fund—VC Fund III and VC Entrepreneurs Fund III); however, there are also cases where firms will fund out of two completely separate funds, say VC Fund III and VC Fund IV. These are called *cross-fund investments*. Typically, you'll see this when the first fund (Fund III) is underreserved and the second fund (Fund IV) fills in the gap to help the VC firm as a whole protect its position and provide support for the company.

Cross-fund investing can lead to several problems between the VC firm and its LPs. Cross-fund investing is rarely done from the beginning of an investment, so the later rounds are done at a different price (not always higher) than the earlier rounds. Since the underlying funds almost always have different LP composition and each fund will end up with a different return profile on the exit, the LPs won't be treated economically equally across the investment. In the upside case where the valuation is steadily increasing, this won't matter as everyone will be happy with the positive economic outcome. However, in the downside case, or an upside case where the round that the second fund invests in is a down round, this is a no-win situation for the VC. In this situation, one fund will be disadvantaged over the other and some LPs will end up in a worse situation than they would have been in if the cross-fund investment hadn't happened. And if our friendly VC thinks too hard, the economic conflict will start to melt his brain.

Departing Partners

Most VC firms have a *key man clause* that defines what happens in the case in which a certain number of partners or a specific partner leaves the firm. In some cases, when a firm trips the key man clause, the LPs have the right to suspend the ability of the fund to make new investments or can even shut down the fund. In cases where a partner leaves the firm but doesn't trip the key man clause, there are often contentious issues over firm economics, especially if the firm has been poorly structured, doesn't have appropriate vesting, or has a significant amount of economics in the hands of the departing partner, leaving the other partners with insignificant motivation (at least in their minds) for continuing to actively manage the firm. While the entrepreneur can't impact this, it's important to be sensitive to any potential dynamics in the structure of the firm, especially if the departing partner is the one who sits on your board or has sponsored the investment in your company.

Fiduciary Duties

VCs owe *fiduciary duties*, concurrently and on the same importance level, to their management company, to the GP, to the LP, and to each board that they serve on. Normally, this all works out fine if one is dealing with a credible and legitimate VC firm, but even in the best of cases, these duties can conflict with one another and VCs can find themselves in a fiduciary sandwich. For the entrepreneur, it's important to remember that no matter how much you love your VCs, they answer to other people and have a complex set of formal, legal responsibilities. Some VCs understand this well, are transparent, and have a clearly defined set of internal guidelines when they find themselves in the midst of fiduciary conflicts. Others don't and subsequently act in confusing, complicated, and occasionally difficult ways. More annoyingly to the VCs who understand this well, some VCs pontificate about their fiduciary duties while not really knowing what to do. If you ever feel uncomfortable with the dynamic, remember that your legal counsel represents your company and can help you cut through the noise to understand what is really going on.

Implications for the Entrepreneur

VCs' motivations and financial incentives will show up in many ways that may affect their judgment or impact them emotionally, especially in times of difficult or pivotal decisions for a company. Don't be blind to the issues that affect your investment partners. More importantly, don't be afraid to discuss these issues with them; an uncomfortable, yet open discussion today could save you the trauma of a surprise and company-impacting interaction later.

Negotiation Tactics

Regardless of how much you know about term sheets, you still need to be able to negotiate a good deal. We've found that most people, including many lawyers, are weak negotiators. Fortunately for our portfolio company executives, they can read about everything we know online and in this book, so hopefully in addition to being better negotiators, they now know all of our moves and can negotiate more effectively against us.

There are plenty of treatises on negotiations; however, this chapter walks through some negotiation tactics that have worked well for us over the years. Although this book is primarily about financings, we'll talk about a range of negotiation tactics that you can use in your life, and we illustrate some of the different types of characters you'll probably meet along the way.

What Really Matters?

There are only three things that matter when negotiating a financing: achieving a good and fair result, not killing your personal relationship getting there, and understanding the deal that you are striking.

It has been said that a good deal means neither party is happy. This might be true in litigation or acquisitions, but if neither party is happy following the closing of a venture financing, then you have a real problem. Remember, the financing is only the beginning of the relationship and a small part at that. Building the company together while having a productive and good relationship is what matters. A great starting point is for both sides to think they have achieved a fair result and feel lucky to be in business with one another. If you behave poorly during the financing, it's likely that tensions will be strained for some time if the deal actually gets closed. And, if your lawyer behaved badly during the negotiation, it's likely that lawyer will be looking for a new client after the VC joins the board.

The Entrepreneur's Perspective

Your lawyer shouldn't be a jerk in manner or unreasonable in positions, but this doesn't mean you should advise your lawyer to behave in a milquetoast manner during negotiations, especially if he is well versed in venture financings. You need to manage this carefully as the entrepreneur, even if your eyes glaze over at legalese. This is your company and your deal, not your lawyer's.

As for which deal terms matter, we've talked previously about economics and control. We'd suggest that any significant time you are spending negotiating beyond these two core concepts is a waste of time. You can learn a lot about the person you are negotiating with by what that individual focuses on.

Pick a few things that really matter—the valuation, stock option pool, liquidation preferences, board, and voting controls—and be done with it. The cliché "you never make money on terms" is especially true outside of a few key ones that we've dwelled on already. The good karma that will attach to you from the other side (assuming they aren't jerks) will be well worth it.

Preparing for the Negotiation

The single biggest mistake people make during negotiation is a lack of preparation. It's incredible to us that people will walk blindly into a negotiation when so much is on the line. And this isn't just about venture deals, as we've seen this behavior in all types of negotiations.

Many people don't prepare because they feel they don't know what they should prepare for. We'll give you some ideas, but realize that you probably do know how to negotiate better than you think. You already negotiate many times a day during your interactions in life, but most people generally just do it and don't think too hard about it. If you have a spouse, child, auto mechanic, domesticated animal, or any friends, chances are that you have dozens of negotiations every day.

When you are going to negotiate your financing (or anything, really), have a plan. Have key things that you want, understand which terms you are willing to concede, and know when you are willing to walk away. If you try to determine this during the negotiation, your emotions are likely to get the best of you and you'll make mistakes. Always have a plan.

Next, spend some time beforehand getting to know whom you are dealing with. Some people (like us) are so easy to find that you can Google us and know just about everything we think. If we openly state that we think people who negotiate registration rights in a term sheets are idiots (which we do), then why on earth would you or your lawyer make a big deal about it? This being said, more than 50 percent of the term sheet markups we get from lawyers have requested changes to the registration rights section, which makes us instantly look down upon the lawyer and know that the entrepreneur isn't the one running the show.

If you get to know the other side ahead of time, you might also be able to play to their strengths, weaknesses, biases, curiosities, and insecurities. The saying "knowledge is power" applies here. And remember, just because you can gain the upper hand in using this type of knowledge doesn't mean that you have to, but it will serve as a security blanket and might be necessary if things turn south.

One thing to remember: everyone has an advantage over everyone else in all negotiations. There might be a David to the Goliath, but even David knew a few things that the big man didn't. Life is the same way. Figure out your superpower and your adversary's kryptonite.

If you are a first-time, 20-something entrepreneur negotiating a term sheet against a 40-something, well-weathered, and experienced VC, what possible advantage could you have on the VC? The VC clearly understands the terms better. The VC also has a ton of market knowledge. And let's assume that this VC is the only credible funding source that you have. Sounds pretty bleak, right?

Well, yes, but don't despair. There is one immediate advantage that you probably have: time. If we generalize, it's easy to come up with a scenario of the VC having a family and lots of portfolio companies and investors to deal with. You, on the other hand, have one singular focus: your company and this negotiation. You can afford to make the process a longer one than the VC might want. In fact, most experienced VCs really hate this part of the process and will bend on terms in order to aid efficiency, although some won't and will nitpick every point (we'll deal with those folks later). Perhaps you'll want to set up your negotiation call at the end of the day, right before the VC's dinner. Or maybe you'll sweetly ask your VC to explain a host of terms that you "don't understand" and further put burdens on the VC's time. Think this doesn't happen? After we gave this advice to some of the TechStars (see www.techstars.org) teams in 2009, one of the teams waited until two hours before Jason left on vacation to negotiate the term sheet we gave them. Jason didn't even recognize this as their strategy and figured it was bad luck with timing. As a result, he faced time pressure that was artificially manufactured by a 20-something first-time entrepreneur. Nice job, Alex.

There are advantages all over the place. Is your VC a huge Stanford fan? Chat him up and find out if he has courtside seats to the game. Is your VC into a charity that you care about? Use this information to connect with your VC so he becomes more sympathetic. While simple things like this are endless, what matters is that you have a plan, know the other side, and consider what natural advantages you have. In a perfect world, you won't have to use any of these tools, but if you need them and don't bring them to the actual negotiation, it's your loss.

The Entrepreneur's Perspective

Your biggest advantage is to have a solid Plan B—lots of interest and competition for your deal. VCs will fold like a house of cards on all peripheral terms if you have another comparable quality VC waiting in the wings to work with you.

A Brief Introduction to Game Theory

Everyone has a natural negotiating style. These styles have analogues that can work either well or poorly in trying to achieve a negotiated result. It's important to understand how certain styles work well together, how some conflict, and how some have inherent advantages over one another.

Before we delve into that, let's spend a little time on basic game theory. *Game theory* is a mathematical theory that deals with strategies for maximizing gains and minimizing losses within prescribed constraints, such as the rules of a card game. Game theory is widely applied in the solution of various decision-making problems, such as those of military strategy and business policy.

Game theory states that there are rules underlying situations that affect how these situations will be played out. These rules are independent of the humans involved and will predict and change how humans interact within the constructs of the situation. Knowing what these invisible rules are is of major importance when entering into any type of negotiation.

The most famous of all games is the prisoner's dilemma, which you've seen many times if you've ever watched a cop show on television. The simple form, as described in the Stanford Encyclopedia of Philosophy (http://plato.stanford.edu/entries/prisoner-dilemma/#Sym2t2PDOrdPay), follows:

> Tanya and Cinque have been arrested for robbing the Hibernia Savings Bank and placed in separate isolation cells. Both care much more about their personal freedom than about the welfare of their accomplice. A clever prosecutor makes the following offer to each. "You may choose to confess or remain silent. If you confess and your accomplice remains silent I will drop all charges against you and use your testimony to ensure that your accomplice does serious time. Likewise, if your accomplice confesses while you remain silent, they will go free while you do the time. If you both confess I get two convictions, but I'll see to it that you both get early parole. If you both remain silent, I'll have to settle for token sentences on firearms possession charges. If you wish to confess, you must leave a note with the jailer before my return tomorrow morning."

The classic prisoner's dilemma can be summarized as shown in the following table.

Classic Prisoner's Dilemma

	Prisoner B Stays Silent	Prisoner B Betrays
Prisoner A Stays Silent	Each serves 8 months	Prisoner A: 12 years Prisoner B: goes free
Prisoner A Betrays	Prisoner A: goes free Prisoner B: 12 years	Each serves 5 years

What's fascinating about this is that there is a fundamental rule in this game that demonstrates why two people might not cooperate with one another, even if it is clearly in their best interests to do so.

If the two prisoners cooperate, the outcome is best, in the aggregate, for both of them. They each get eight months of jail time and walk away. But the game forces different behavior. Regardless of what the co-conspirator chooses (silence versus betrayal), each player always receives a lighter sentence by betraying the other. In other words, no matter what the other guy does, you are always better off by ratting him out.

The other rule to this game is that it is a *single-play game*. In other words, the participants play the game once and their fate is cast. Other games are *multiplay games*. For instance, there is a lot of interesting game theory about battlegrounds. If you are in one trench fighting and we are in another, game theory would suggest that we would not fight at night, on weekends, on holidays, and during meals. Why not? It would seem logical that if we know you are sleeping, it's the absolute best time to attack.

Well, it's not, unless we can completely take you out with one strike. Otherwise, you'll most likely start attacking *us* during dinner, on holidays, or while we are watching *Mad Men*. And then not only are we still fighting, but now we've both lost our free time. This tit-for-tat strategy is what keeps multiplay games at equilibrium. If you don't mess with us during our lunch break, we won't mess with you during yours. And everyone is better off. But if you do mess with us, we'll continue to mess with you until you are nice to us again.

When you are considering which game you are playing, consider not only whether there are forces at work that influence the decisions being made, like the prisoner's dilemma, but also how many times a decision will be made. Is this a one-shot deal, or will this game repeat itself, lending increased importance to precedent and reputation?

Negotiating in the Game of Financings

A venture financing is one of the easiest games there is. First, you really can have a win-win outcome where everyone is better off. Second, you don't negotiate in a vacuum like your hypothetical fellow criminal co-conspirator. Last, and most important, this is not a single-instance game. Therefore, reputation and the fear of tit-for-tat retaliation are real considerations.

Since the VC and entrepreneur will need to spend a lot of time together postinvestment, the continued relationship makes it important to look at the financing as just one negotiation in a very long, multiplay game. Doing anything that would give the other party an incentive to retaliate in the future is not a wise, or rational, move.

Furthermore, for the VC, this financing is but one of many that the VC will hope to complete. Therefore, the VC should be thinking about reputational factors that extend well beyond this particular interaction. With the maturation of the VC industry, it's easy to get near-perfect information on most VCs. Having a negative reputation can be fatal to a VC in the long run.

Not all VCs recognize that each negotiation isn't a single-round, winner-take-all game. Generally, the more experience VCs have, the better their perspective is, but this lack of a longer-term view is not limited to junior VCs. While we'll often see this behavior more from the lawyers representing the VCs or the entrepreneurs, we also see it from the business principals. When we run across people like this, at a minimum we lose a lot of respect for them and occasionally decide not to do business with them. When you encounter VCs who either have a reputation for or are acting as though every negotiation is a single-round, winner-take-all game, you should be very cautious.

The Entrepreneur's Perspective

One successful negotiating tactic is to ask VCs up front, before the term sheet shows up, what the three most important terms are in a financing for them. You should know and be prepared to articulate your top three wants as well. This conversation can set the stage for how you think about negotiating down the road, and it can be helpful to you when you are in the heat of a negotiation. If the VCs are pounding hard on a point that is not one of their stated top three, it's much easier to call them out on that fact and note that they are getting most or all of their main points.

Game theory is also useful because of the other types of negotiations you'll have. For instance, if you decide to sell your company, your acquisition discussions can be similar to the prisoner's dilemma as presented earlier. Customer negotiations usually take on the feeling of a single-round game, despite any thoughts to the contrary about partnerships. And litigation almost always takes the form of a single-round game, even when the parties will have ongoing relationships beyond the resolution of the litigation.

Remember, you can't change the game you are in, but you can judge people who play poorly within it. And having a game theory lens to view the other side is very useful.

Negotiating Styles and Approaches

Every person has a natural negotiating style that is often the part of your personality that you adopt when you are dealing with conflict. Few people have truly different modes for negotiation, but that doesn't mean you can't practice having a range of different behaviors that depend on the situation you are in.

Most good negotiators know where they are comfortable, but also know how to play upon and against other people's natural styles. Following are some of the personalities you'll meet and how you might want to best work with them.

The Bully *(aka UAW Negotiator)*

The bully negotiates by yelling and screaming, forcing issues, and threatening the other party. Most folks who are bullies aren't that smart and don't really understand the issues; rather, they try to win by force. There are two ways to deal with bullies: punch them in the nose or mellow out so much that you sap their strength. If you can outbully the bully, go for it. But if you are wrong, then you've probably ignited a volcano. Unlike the children's playground, getting hit by a bully during a negotiation generally doesn't hurt; so unless this is your natural negotiating style, our advice is to chill out as your adversary gets hotter.

The Nice Guy *(aka Used-Car Salesman)*

Whenever you interact with this pleasant person, you feel like he's trying to sell you something. Often you aren't sure that you want what he's selling. When you say no, the nice guy will either be openly disappointed or will keep on smiling at you just like the audience at a Tony Robbins event. In their world, life is great as long as you acquiesce to their terms (or buy this clean 2006 Chrysler Sebring).

As the negotiation unfolds, the nice guy is increasingly hard to pin down on anything. While the car salesman always needs to go talk to his manager, the nice-guy negotiator regularly responds with "Let me consider that and get back to you." While the nice guy doesn't yell at you like the bully, it's often frustrating that you can never get a real answer or seemingly make progress. Our advice is to be clear and direct and don't get worn down, as the nice guys will happily talk to you all day. If all else fails, don't be afraid to toss a little bully into the mix on your side to move things forward.

The Technocrat *(aka Pocket Protector Guy)*

This is the technical nerd guy. Although he won't yell at you like the bully and you don't wonder if there is a real human being behind the façade like you do with the nice guy, you will feel like you are in endless detail hell. The technocrat has a billion issues and has a hard time deciding what's really important, since to him everything is important for some reason. Our advice is to grin and bear it and perhaps play Farmville while you are listening to the other side drag on. Technocrats tend to cause you to lose your focus during the negotiation. Make sure you don't by remembering what you care about and conceding the other points. But make sure you cover all the points together, as the technocrat will often negotiate every point from scratch, not taking into consideration the give-and-take of each side during the negotiation.

The Wimp *(aka George McFly)*

The wimp may sound like the perfect dance partner here, but he has his own issues. Our bet is that you can take his wallet pretty easily during the negotiation, but if you get too good a deal it will come back to haunt you. And then you get to live with him on your board of directors once you close your financing. With the wimp, you end up negotiating both sides of the deal. Sometimes this is harder than having a real adversary.

The Curmudgeon *(aka Archie Bunker)*

With the curmudgeon, everything you negotiate sucks. No matter what you arrive at is horrible, and every step along the way during the negotiation will feel like a dentist tugging on a tight molar at the back of your mouth. Unlike the bully, the curmudgeon won't yell; and unlike the nice guy, he's never happy. While it'll seem like he doesn't care too much about the details, he's just never happy with any position you are taking. The curmudgeon is also not a wimp; he's been around the block before and will remind you of that every chance he gets. In a lot of ways, the curmudgeon is like a cranky grandfather. If you are patient, upbeat, and tolerant, you'll eventually get what you want, but you'll never really please him because everyone pisses him off.

The Entrepreneur's Perspective

You learn a lot about a person in a negotiation. This is one argument for doing as much of the detailed negotiation before signing a term sheet that includes a no-shop clause in it. If you find that your potential investor is a jerk to you in negotiating your deal, you may want to think twice about this person becoming a board member and member of your inner circle.

Always Be Transparent

What about the normal dude? You know, the transparent, nice, smart, levelheaded person you hope to meet on the other side of the table? Though they exist, everyone has some inherent styles that will find their way into the negotiation, especially if pressed or negotiations aren't going well. Make sure you know which styles you have so you won't surprise yourself with a sudden outburst. You'll also see a lot of these behaviors come out real-time in board meetings when things aren't going quite as well as hoped.

If you are capable of having multiple negotiating personalities, which should you favor? We'd argue that in a negotiation that has reputational and relationship value, try to be the most transparent and easygoing that you can be, to let the other person inside your thinking and get to know you for who you really are. If you are playing a single-round game, like an acquisition negotiation with a party you don't ever expect to do business with again, do like Al Davis says: "Just win, baby." As in sports, don't ever forget that a good tactic is to change your game plan suddenly to keep the other side on their toes.

Collaborative Negotiation versus Walk-Away Threats

Of all the questions we get regarding negotiations, the most common is when to walk away from a deal. Most people's blood pressure ticks up a few points with the thought of walking away, especially after you've invested a lot of time and energy (especially emotional energy) in a negotiation. In considering whether to walk away from a negotiation, preparation is key here—know what your walk-away point is before starting the negotiation so it's a rational and deliberate decision rather than an emotional one made in the heat of the moment.

When determining your walk-away position, consider your *best alternative to negotiated agreement*, also known in business school circles as *BATNA*. Specifically, what is your backup plan if you aren't successful reaching an agreement? The answer to this varies wildly depending on the circumstances. In a financing, if you are lucky, your backup plan may be accepting your second-favorite term sheet from another VC. It could mean bootstrapping your company and forgoing a financing. Understanding BATNA is important in any negotiation, such as an acquisition (walk away as a stand-alone company), litigation (settle versus go to court), and customer contract (walk away rather than get stuck in a bad deal).

Before you begin any negotiation, make sure you know where your overall limits are, as well as your limits on each key point. If you've thought this through in advance, you'll know when someone is trying to move you past one of these boundaries. It's also usually obvious when someone tries to pretend they are at a boundary when they really aren't. Few people are able to feign true conviction.

At some point in some negotiation, you'll find yourself up against the wall or being pushed into a zone that is beyond where you are willing to go. In this situation, tell the other party there is no deal, and walk away. As you walk away, be very clear with what your walk-away point is so the other party will be able to reconsider their position. If you are sincere in walking away and the other party is interested enough in a deal, they'll likely be back at the table at some point and will offer you something that you can stomach. If they don't reengage, the deal wasn't meant to be.

Depending on the type of person you are negotiating with, the VC either will be sensitive to your boundaries or will force you outside these boundaries where BATNA will come into effect. If this is happening regularly during your financing negotiation, think hard about whether this is a VC that you want to be working with, as this VC is likely playing a single-round game in a relationship that will have many rounds and lots of ups and downs along the way.

Finally, don't ever make a threat during a negotiation that you aren't willing to back up. If you bluff and aren't willing to back up your position, your bargaining position is forever lost in this negotiation. The 17th time we hear "and that's our final offer," we know that there's another, better offer coming if we just hold out for number 18.

Building Leverage and Getting to Yes

Besides understanding the issues and knowing how to deal with the other party, there are certain things that you can do to increase your negotiation leverage. In a VC financing, the best way to gain leverage is to have competing term sheets from different VCs.

If you happen to be lucky enough to have several interested parties, this will be the single biggest advantage in getting good deal terms. However, it's a tricky balance dealing with multiple parties at the same time. You have to worry about issues of transparency and timing and, if you play them incorrectly, you might find yourself in a situation where no one wants to work with you.

The Entrepreneur's Perspective

As I mentioned earlier, having a solid Plan B (and a Plan C, and a Plan D . . .) is one of your most effective weapons during the negotiation process. It's helpful to be reasonably transparent about that fact to all prospective investors. While it's a good practice to withhold some information, such as the names of the other potential investors with whom you're speaking since there is no reason to enable two VCs to talk about your deal behind your back, telling investors that you have legitimate interest from other firms will serve you very well in terms of speeding the process along and improving your end result.

For starters, pay attention to timing. You'll want to try to drive each VC to deliver a term sheet to you in roughly the same time frame. This pacing can be challenging since there will be uncomfortable days when you'll end up slow rolling one party while you seek to speed up the process of another firm. This is hard to do, but if you can get VCs to approve a financing around the same time, you're in a much stronger position than if you have one term sheet in hand that you are trying to use to generate additional term sheets.

Once you've received a term sheet from a VC, you can use this to motivate action from other VCs, but you have to walk a fine line between oversharing and being too secretive. We prefer when entrepreneurs are up front, tell us that they have other interests, and let us know where in the process they are. We never ask to see other term sheets, and we'd recommend that you don't ever show your actual term sheets to other investors. More important, you should never disclose whom you are talking to, as one of the first emails most interested VCs will send after hearing about other VCs who are interested in a deal is something like "Hey, I hear you are interested in investing in X—want to share notes?" As a result, you probably no longer have a competitive situation between the two VCs, as they will now talk about your deal and in many cases talk about teaming up. The exception, of course, is when you want them to team up and join together in a syndicate.

At the end of the day, if you have multiple term sheets, most of the deal terms will collapse into the same range (usually entrepreneur favorable), and the only real things you'll be negotiating are valuation and board control. You can signal quite effectively what your other options might be. Whatever you do, don't sign a term sheet and then pull a Brett Favre and change your mind the next day. The startup ecosystem is small and word travels fast. Reputation is important.

Another strategy that can help you build leverage is to anchor on certain terms. Anchoring means to pick a few points, state clearly what you want, and then stick to your guns. If you anchor on positions that are reasonable while still having a little flexibility to give in the negotiation, you will likely get close to what you want as long as you are willing to trade away other points that aren't as important to you.

Although you should try to pace the negotiation, you should do this only after the VC has offered up the first term sheet. Never provide a term sheet to a VC, especially with a price attached, since if you do you've just capped what you can expect to get in the deal. You are always in a stronger position to react to what the VC offers, especially when you have multiple options. However, once you've gotten a term sheet, you should work hard to control the pace of the ensuing negotiation.

As with any type of negotiation, it helps to feed the ego of your partner. Figure out what the other side wants to hear and try to please them. People tend to reciprocate niceties. For example, if you are dealing with technocrats, engage them in depth on some of the deal points, even if the points don't matter to you, in order to make them happy and help them feel like you are playing their game.

When you are leading the negotiation, we highly recommend that you have a strategy about the order in which you will address the points. Your options are to address them either in the order that they are laid out in the term sheet or in some other random order of your choosing. In general, once you are a skilled negotiator, going in order is more effective, as you won't reveal which points matter most to you. Often experienced negotiators will try to get agreement on a point-by-point basis in order to prevent the other party from looking holistically at the process and determining whether a fair deal is being achieved. This strategy really works only if you have a lot of experience, and it can really backfire on you if the other party is more experienced and takes control of the discussion. Instead of being on the giving end of a divide-and-conquer strategy, you'll be on the receiving end of death by a thousand cuts.

Unless you are a very experienced negotiator, we suggest an order where you start with some important points that you think you can get to yes quickly. This way, both parties will feel good that they are making progress toward a deal. Maybe it's liquidation preferences or the stock option plan allocation. Then dive into the minutiae. Valuation is probably the last subject to address, as you'll most likely get closure on other terms but have a couple of different rounds of discussion on valuation. It is completely normal for some terms to drag out longer than others.

Things Not to Do

There are a few things that you'll never want to do when negotiating a financing for your company. As we stated earlier, don't present your term sheet to a VC. In addition to signaling inexperience, you get no benefit by playing your hand first since you have no idea what the VC will offer you. The likely result is either you'll end up starting in a worse place than the VC would have offered or you'll put silly terms out there that will make you look like a rookie. If your potential funding partner tells you to propose the terms, be wary, as it's an indication that you are talking to either someone who isn't a professional VC or someone who is professionally lazy.

The Entrepreneur's Perspective

You should never make an offer first. There's no reason to, unless you have another concrete one on the table. Why run the risk of aiming too low?

Next, make sure you know when to talk and when to listen. If you remember nothing else about this section, remember this: you can't lose a deal point if you don't open your mouth. Listening gives you further information about the other party including what advantages you have over them (e.g., do they have a Little League baseball game to coach in an hour?) and which negotiation styles they are most comfortable with.

The Entrepreneur's Perspective

As the old cliché goes, there's a reason you have two ears and one mouth. When you are negotiating, try to listen more than you talk, especially at the beginning of the negotiation.

If the other party is controlling the negotiation, don't address deal points in order of the legal paper. This is true of all negotiations, not just financings. If you allow a person to address each point and try to get to closure before moving on to the next point, you will lose sight of the deal as a whole. While you might feel like the resolution on each point is reasonable, when you reflect on the entire deal you may be unhappy. If a party forces you into this mode, don't concede points. Listen and let the other party know that you'll consider their position after you hear all of their comments to the document. Many lawyers are trained to do exactly this—to kill you softly point by point.

A lot of people rely on the same arguments over and over again when negotiating. People who negotiate regularly, including many VCs and lawyers, try to convince the other side to acquiesce by stating,

"That's the way it is because it's market." We love hearing the market argument because then we know that our negotiating partner is a weak negotiator. Saying that "it's market" is like your parents telling you, "Because I said so," and you responding, "But everyone's doing it." These are elementary negotiating tactics that should have ended around the time you left for college.

In the world of financings, you'll hear this all the time. Rather than getting frustrated, recognize that it's not a compelling argument since the concept of market terms isn't the sole justification for a negotiation position. Instead, probe on why the market condition applies to you. In many cases, the other party won't be able to justify it and, if they can't make the argument, you'll immediately have the higher ground.

The Entrepreneur's Perspective

Understanding market terms and whether they apply to your situation is important. You can quickly get context on this by talking to other entrepreneurs in similar positions. Remember, you do only a few of these deals in your lifetime, and your VC does them for a living. Understand what market really is, and you'll be able to respond to an assertion that something is market with fact rather than with emotion.

Finally, never assume that the other side has the same ethical code as you. This isn't a comment against VCs or lawyers; rather, it's a comment about life and pertains to every type of negotiation you'll find yourself involved in. Everyone has a different acceptable ethical code and it can change depending on the context of the negotiations. For instance, if you were to lie about the current state of a key customer to a prospective VC and it was discovered before the deal closed, you'd most likely find your deal blown up. Or perhaps the deal would close, but you'd be fired afterward and it's likely that some of your peers would hear about it. As a result, both parties (VC and entrepreneur) have solid motivation to behave in an ethical way during a financing. Note that this is directly in contrast to most behavior, at least between lawyers, in a litigation context where lies and half-truths are an acceptable part of that game. Regardless of the specific negotiation context, make sure you know the ethical code of the party you are negotiating against.

Great Lawyers versus Bad Lawyers versus No Lawyers

Regardless of how much you think you know or how much you've read, hire a great lawyer. In many cases you will be the least experienced person around the negotiating table. VCs negotiate for a living, and a great lawyer on your side will help balance things out. When choosing a lawyer, make sure he not only understands the deal mechanics, but also has a style that you like working with and that you are comfortable sitting alongside of. This last point can't be overstated—your lawyer is a reflection of you, and if you choose a lawyer who is inexperienced, is ineffective, or behaves inconsistently, it will reflect poorly on you and decrease your negotiating credibility.

So choose a great lawyer, but make sure you know what *great* means. Ask multiple entrepreneurs you respect whom they use. Check around your local entrepreneurial community for the lawyers with the best reputations. Don't limit your exploration to billing rates, responsiveness, and intellect, but also check style and how contentious negotiations were resolved. Furthermore, it's completely acceptable to ask your VC before and after the funding what the VC's thoughts are about your lawyer.

The Entrepreneur's Perspective

Choosing a great lawyer doesn't mean hiring an expensive lawyer from a firm that your VC knows or recommends. Often for startups, going to a top-tier law firm means dealing with a second-tier or very junior lawyer, not well supervised, with high billing rates. You can hire a smaller firm with lower rates and partner attention just as well; but be sure to do your homework on them, make sure they're experienced in dealing with venture financings, and get references—even from VCs they've negotiated against in the past.

Can You Make a Bad Deal Better?

Let's say you screw up and negotiate a bad deal. You had only one term sheet, the VC was a combination bully and technocrat, and you are now stuck with deal terms that you don't love. Should you spend all of your time being depressed? Nope, there are plenty of ways to fix things after the fact that most entrepreneurs never think about.

First of all, until an exit—either an acquisition or an IPO—many of the terms don't matter much. But more important, if you plan to raise another round led by a new investor, you have a potential ally at the time to clean up the things you negotiated poorly in the first investment. The new VC will be motivated to make sure you and your team are happy (assuming the company is performing), and if you talk to your new potential financing partner about issues that are troubling you, in many cases the new VC will concentrate on trying to bring these back into balance in the new financing.

In the case where a new VC doesn't lead the next round, you still have the option of sitting down with your current VCs after you've had some run time together (again, assuming success). We've been involved in numerous cases in which these were very constructive conversations that resulted in entrepreneur-friendly modifications to a deal.

Finally, you can wait until the exit and deal with your issues then. Most acquisition negotiations include a heavy focus on retention dynamics for the management team going forward, and there are often cases of reallocating some of the proceeds from the investors to management. The style of your VCs will impact how this plays out. If they are playing a single-round game with the negotiation and they don't really care what happens after the deal closes, they will be inflexible. However, if they want to be in a position to invest with you again in the future, they'll take a top-down view of the situation and be willing to work through modifications to the deal terms to reallocate some consideration to management and employees, especially in a retention situation for the acquirer.

Recognize, however, that this dynamic cuts both ways—many acquirers take the approach that they want to recut the economics in favor of the entrepreneur. Remember that as an entrepreneur you signed up for the deal you currently have with your investors and you have a corresponding responsibility to them. If you end up playing a single-round game with your investors where you team up with the acquirer, you run the risk of blowing up both the acquisition and your relationship with your investors. So, be thoughtful, fair, and open with your investors around the incentives and dynamics.

The Entrepreneur's Perspective

Having an open and collaborative approach with your VC in the context of an acquisition may sound a bit like a game of chicken—but it can work. Being clear with your investors about what is important to you and your team early in the negotiation can help set a tone where you and your investors are working together to reach the right deal structure, especially when the acquirer is trying to drive a wedge between you and those investors. A negotiation in a state of plenty is much easier than a negotiation in a state of scarcity.

In our experience, openness in these situations of both the entrepreneur and the VC generally results in much better outcomes. It's hard enough to engage in a negotiation, let alone one in which there are multiple parties in a negotiation at cross-purposes (e.g., acquirer, entrepreneur, and VC). We always encourage entrepreneurs and their VC backers to keep focused on doing what is right for all shareholders in the context of whatever is being offered, and as a result to continue to constructively work through any issues, especially if one party is uncomfortable with where they previously ended up.

11

Raising Money the Right Way

While most people ask themselves "What should I do?" when seeking VC financing, there are also some things that a person should *not* do. Doing any of the following at best makes you look like a rookie (which is okay, we were all rookies once, but you don't want to look like one) and at worst kills any chance that you have of getting funded by the VC you just contacted. We encourage you to avoid doing the following when you are raising money from VCs.

Don't Ask for a Nondisclosure Agreement

Don't ask a VC for a *nondisclosure agreement* (NDA). Although most VCs will respect how unique your idea, innovation, or company is to you, it's likely that they've seen similar things due to the sheer number of business plans that they get. If they sign an NDA regarding any company, they'd likely run afoul of it if they ended up funding a company that you consider a competitor. An NDA will also prevent a VC from talking to other VCs about your company, even ones who might be good co-investors for your financing.

On the other hand, don't be too scared about approaching a reputable VC with your idea without an NDA. The VC industry is small and wouldn't last long if VCs spoke out of turn sharing people's knowledge with one another. And don't think that VCs will steal your idea and start a company, as reputational constraints as well as limits on a VC's time will eliminate this risk in most cases. Though you might occasionally run into a bad actor, do your homework and you'll generally be fine.

Don't Email Carpet Bomb VCs

You might not know VCs personally, but the way to get to know them is not by buying a mailing list and sending personalized spam. And it's not good to hire an investment adviser who will do the same. VCs know when they are getting a personal pitch versus spam, and we don't know any VCs who react well to spam.

Spamming looks lazy. If you didn't take the time to really think about who would be a good funding partner, what does that say about how you run the rest of the business? If you want to contact us, just email us, but make it personal to us.

No Often Means No

While most VCs appreciate persistence, when they say they aren't interested, they usually mean it. We aren't asking you to try again. We might be saying no because your idea isn't personally interesting to us, doesn't fit our current investment themes, or is something that we think is a bad idea—or just because we are too busy. One thing to know is that us saying no doesn't mean that your idea is stupid; it just means it isn't for us.

Don't Ask for a Referral If You Get a No

VCs get a lot of inbound email from entrepreneurs (and bankers and lawyers) pitching new investments. At our firm, we try to look at all of them and always attempt to respond within a day. We say no to most of them, but we are happy to be on the receiving end of them (and encourage you, dear reader, to send us email anytime).

When we say no, we try to do it quickly and clearly. We try to give an explanation, although we don't attempt to argue or debate our reason. We are sure that many of the things we say no to will get funded and some will become incredibly successful companies. That's okay with us; even if we say no, we are still rooting for you.

However, if we say no, please don't respond and ask us to refer you to someone. You don't really want us to do this, even if you don't realize it. By referring you to someone else, at some level we are implicitly endorsing you. At the same time, we just told you that we are not interested in exploring funding your deal. These two constructs are in conflict with each other. The person we refer you to will immediately ask us if we are interested in funding your deal.

We are now in the weird position of implicitly endorsing you on one side, while rejecting you on the other. This isn't necessarily comfortable for us, and it's useless to you, as the likelihood of the person we have just referred you to taking you seriously is very low. In fact, you'd probably have a better shot at it if we weren't in the mix in the first place!

The Entrepreneur's Perspective

There's one exception to it not being suitable to ask for a referral. If you have a relationship with the VC (e.g., it's not a cold request), ask why the answer is no. If the response to that question is something about the VC firm rather than your company (e.g., "You're too small for us," or "One of our portfolio companies is too competitive"), then you may ask for a referral to another firm that might be a better fit. However, be respectful here—if the VC doesn't want to make a referral, don't push it.

Somewhere in a parallel universe, someone trained a bunch of us (probably Networking 101 or at a Zig Ziglar seminar) to always "ask for something" when you hear a "no" (e.g., keep the conversation going, get a referral, or try a different question). However, there are cases where this isn't useful—to you.

Don't Be a Solo Founder

Outside of some very isolated examples, most entrepreneurs will have little chance of raising money unless they have a team. A team can be a team of two, but the solo entrepreneur raising money can be a red flag.

First, no single person can do everything. We've not met anyone who can do absolutely everything from product vision to executing on a plan, engineering development, marketing, sales, operations, and so on. There are just too many mission-critical tasks in getting a successful company launched. You will be much happier if you have a partner to back you up.

Second, it's not a good sign if you can't get others to get excited about your plan. It's hard enough to get VCs to write checks to fund your company; if you can't find other team members with the same passion and beliefs as you have, this is a warning sign to anyone who might want to fund your company.

Last, if you don't have a team, what is the VC investing in? Often, the team executing the idea is more important than the idea itself. Most VCs will tell you that they've made money on grade B ideas with grade A teams but that many A ideas were left in the dustbin due to a substandard team.

The one exception would be a repeat entrepreneur. If the venture fund has had a good experience with an entrepreneur before and believes they can build a solid team postfunding, then the person has a chance to get funded as a solo entrepreneur.

Don't Overemphasize Patents

Don't rely on patents. We see a lot of entrepreneurs basically hinge their entire company's worth on their patent strategy. If you are in biotech or medical devices, this might be entirely appropriate. When you are working on software, realize that patents are, at best, defensive weapons for others coming after you. Creating a successful software business is about having a great idea and executing well, not about patents, in our opinion.

In fact, we wish that all business method and software patents didn't exist (and make a lot of noise about this on our personal blogs at www.jasonmendelson.com and www.feld.com), so if you think you are winning us over for investment in a software company by relying on your patent portfolio, you aren't. Instead, you just proved to us that you did no homework on us as investors and don't really understand the value of patents versus a rock-star management team and amazing software engineers going after a big idea.

CHAPTER

Issues at Different Financing Stages

Not all financings are created equal. This is especially true when you factor in the different stages that your company will evolve through over its lifetime. Each financing stage—seed, early, mid, and later stage—has different key issues to focus on.

Seed Deals

While seed deals have the lowest legal costs and usually involve the least contentious negotiations, seed deals often allow for the most potential mistakes. Given how important precedent is in future financings, if you reach a bad outcome on a specific term, you might be stuck with it for the life of your company. Ironically, we've seen more cases where the entrepreneur got too good a deal instead of a bad one.

What's wrong with getting great terms? If you can't back them up with performance when you raise your next round, you may find yourself in a difficult position with your original investor. For example, assume you are successful getting a valuation that is significantly ahead of where your business currently is. If your next round isn't at a higher valuation, you are going to be diluting your original shareholders—the investors who took a big risk to fund you during the seed stage. Either you'll have to make them whole or, worse, they'll vote to block the new financing. This is especially true in cases with unsophisticated seed investors who were expecting that, no matter what, the next round price would be higher.

Early Stage

As with seed deals, precedent is important in early stage deals. In our experience, the terms you get in your first VC-led round will carry over to all future financings. One item that can haunt you forever is the liquidation preference. While it may not seem like a big deal to agree to a participating preferred feature given that most early stage rounds aren't large dollar amounts, if you plan to raise larger rounds one day, these participation features can drastically reduce return characteristics for the common stockholders.

Another term to pay extra attention to at the early stage is the protective provisions. You will want to try to collapse the protective provisions so that all preferred stockholders, regardless of series, vote together on them. If by your second round of financing you are stuck with two separate votes for protective provisions, you are most likely stuck with a structure that will give each series of stock a separate vote and thus separate blocking rights. This can be a real pain to manage when you have multiple lead investors in multiple rounds that each have their own motivations to deal with.

Mid and Late Stages

Later stage deals tend to have two tough issues—board and voting control. The voting control issues in the early stage deals are only amplified as you wrestle with how to keep control of your board when each lead investor per round wants a board seat. Either you can increase your board size to seven, nine, or more people (which usually effectively kills a well-functioning board), or more likely the board will be dominated by investors. If your investors are well behaved, this might not be a problem; but you'll still be serving a lot of food at board meetings.

There isn't necessarily a good answer here. Unless you have massive negotiating power in a super-hot company, you are likely to give a board seat to each lead investor in each round. If you raise subsequent rounds, unless you've worked hard to manage this early, your board will likely expand and in many cases the founders will lose control of the board.

The Entrepreneur's Perspective

There are ways to mitigate issues of board and voting control, such as placing a cap (early on) on the number or percentage of directors who can be VCs as opposed to independent directors, preemptively offering observer rights to any director who is dethroned, or establishing an executive committee of the board that can meet whenever and wherever you'd like without everyone else around the table.

The last thing to consider is valuation. Much like issues that we've seen in seed deals, there have been some deals that have been too good and have forced the VCs to hold out for a huge exit price. The net effect was that by raising money at such a high valuation, the entrepreneurs forfeited the ability to sell the company at a price they would have been happy with, because of the inherent valuation-creation desires of the VCs who paid such a high price.

Other Approaches to Early Stage Deals

We've spent a lot of time on classic preferred stock financings, but there are other options. Over the past few years we've seen the proliferation of *seed preferred* or *light preferred* term sheets as well as the use of *convertible debt* in seed and early stage deals. Let's take a quick look at these.

In a seed or light preferred deal, the parties are agreeing to a class of preferred stock that doesn't have all the protections and rights that typical preferred shareholders have. Why would investors agree to this? Well, for one, the company may be raising money from angel investors who don't require things like a board seat or protective provisions. In fact, it might not be appropriate given their financial commitment for these investors to have these rights.

Due to IRS tax regulation 409A (Section 409A is an IRS rule that we will discuss later), you don't want to sell common stock to investors; otherwise, you'll peg the price of your common stock at a higher valuation than you want. Since you want to incentivize your early employees by granting them low-priced common stock options, a light preferred deal is a way to sell stock to investors while maintaining a low regular common stock price with which to grant stock options.

Letters of Intent—The Other Term Sheet

There is another type of term sheet that is important in an entrepreneur's life—the *letter of intent* (LOI). Hopefully, one day you'll receive one from a potential acquirer that will lead to fame, riches, and happiness. Or at least you'll get a new business card on heavier card stock.

Typically the first formal step by a company that wants to acquire yours is for it to issue a letter of intent. This sometimes delightful and usually nonbinding document (except for things like a no-shop agreement) is also known as an indication of interest (IOI), memorandum of understanding (MOU), and even occasionally a term sheet.

As with our friend the term sheet, there are some terms that matter a lot and others that don't. Once again there are plenty of mysterious words that experienced deal makers always know how and where to sprinkle so that they can later say, "But X implies Y," often resulting in much arguing between lawyers. We've had LOIs get done in a couple of hours and had others take several months to get signed. As with any negotiation, experience, knowledge, and understanding matter. The LOI negotiation is usually a first taste of the actual negotiating style you will experience from the other party.

To keep things straightforward, we are going to focus on explaining the typical case of a two-party transaction between a buyer and a seller, which we'll refer to as an *acquisition*. As with many things in life, there are often more complex transactions, including three or more parties, but we'll save that for a different book.

By the time the buyer presents the seller with an LOI, there have been meetings, discussions, dinners, expensive bottles of wine, lots of conference calls, and an occasional argument. However, the buyer and the seller are still courting so they tend to be on their best behavior. The LOI is typically the first real negotiation and the true icebreaker for the relationship.

In ancient times, when the first LOI was presented, someone crafted an introductory paragraph that started off with something like the following:

> Dear CEO of Seller:
>
> We have greatly enjoyed our conversations to date and are honored to present you with this letter of intent to acquire [Seller's Company]. We look forward to entering into serious discussions over the next several months and reaching an agreement to acquire your company. We'd like to thank you for entertaining our proposal, which follows:

While every company has its own style, most LOIs begin with some variation of this boilerplate paragraph. Of course, you'll find—later in the LOI—a qualifier that states that almost everything in the LOI is nonbinding, including the appearance of civility as part of the negotiation.

Structure of a Deal

As with financings, there are only a couple of things that really matter—in this case price and structure. Since the first question anyone involved in a deal typically asks is "What is the price?" we'll start there.

Unlike a venture financing in which price is usually pretty straightforward to understand, figuring out the price in an acquisition can be more difficult. There is usually some number floated in early discussions, but this isn't really the actual price since there are a lot of factors that can (and generally will) impact the final price of a deal by the time the negotiations are finished and the deal is closed. It's usually a safe bet to assume that the easy-to-read number on the first page of the LOI is the best-case scenario purchase price. Following is an example of what you might see in a typical LOI.

> Purchase Price/Consideration: $100 million of cash will be paid at closing, $15 million of which will be subject to the terms of the escrow provisions described in paragraph 3 of this Letter of Intent. Working capital of at least $1 million shall be delivered at closing. Forty million dollars of cash will be subject to an earn-out and $10 million of cash will be part of a management retention pool. Buyer will not assume outstanding options to purchase Company Common Stock, and any options to purchase shares of Company Common Stock not exercised prior to the Closing will be terminated as of the Closing. Warrants to purchase shares of Company capital stock not exercised prior to the Closing will be terminated as of the Closing.

Before this paragraph was drafted, it's likely that a number around $150 million was discussed as the purchase price. The first thing that jumps out is the reference to a $15 million *escrow*. The escrow (also known as a *holdback*) is money that the buyer is going to hang on to for some period of time to satisfy any issues that come up postfinancing that are not disclosed in the purchase agreement. In some LOIs we've seen extensive details, whereas each provision of the escrow is spelled out, including the percentage of the holdback, length of time, and *carve-outs* to the indemnity agreement. In other cases, there is mention that "standard escrow and indemnity terms shall apply." We'll discuss specific escrow language later (i.e., you'll have to wait until "paragraph 3"), but it's safe to say two things: first, there is no such thing as standard language and second, whatever the escrow arrangement is, it will decrease the actual purchase price should any claim be brought under it. So clearly the amount and terms of the escrow and indemnity provisions are very important.

Next is the reference to $1 million of working capital. While this might not seem like a big number, it's still $1 million. Many young companies end up with negative working capital at closing (working capital is current assets minus current liabilities) due to debt, deferred revenue, warranty reserves, inventory carry costs, and expenses and fees associated with the deal. As a result, these working capital adjustments directly decrease the purchase price if upon closing (or other predetermined date after the closing) the seller's working capital is less than an agreed-upon amount. Assume that unless the working capital threshold is a slam-dunk situation where the company has clearly complied with this requirement, the determination will be a battle that can have a real impact on the purchase price. In some cases, this can act in the seller's favor to increase the value of the deal if the seller has more working capital on the balance sheet than the buyer requires, but only if the clause around working capital is bidirectional (it's not in this example).

While *earn-outs* sound like a mechanism to increase price, in our experience, they usually are a tool that allows the acquirer to underpay at time of closing and pay full value only if certain hurdles are met in the future. In our example, the acquirer suggested that it was willing to pay $150 million, but is really paying only $100 million with $40 million of the deal subject to an earn-out. We'll cover earn-outs separately since there are a lot of permutations, especially if the seller is receiving stock instead of cash as its consideration.

In our example, the buyer has explicitly carved out $10 million for a management retention pool. This has become common since buyers want to make sure that management has a clear and direct future financial incentive. In this case, it's built into the purchase price (e.g., $150 million). We've found that buyers tend to be split between building it into the purchase price and putting it on top of the purchase price. In either case, it is effectively part of the deal consideration, but is at risk since it'll typically be paid out over several years to the members of management who continue their role at the acquirer. If someone leaves, that portion of the management retention pool tends to vanish into the same place socks lost in the drier go. In addition, it's a move on the part of the buyer to allocate some percentage of the purchase price away from the formal ownership (or capitalization table) of the company as a way of driving an early negotiating wedge between management and the investors.

The Entrepreneur's Perspective

By the time someone is offering you a lot of money to buy your company, you should have good counsel or advisers or independent board members to help you navigate the terms. The structure of the deal is very important. You should be willing to stand behind your *representations and warrantees* with a reasonable 12- to 18-month escrow at a minimum. If you can't, you look like you're hiding something. Management retention pool, networking capital, and earn-outs are just negotiation points around the certainty and price of a deal.

Finally, there are a bunch of words in our example about the buyer not assuming stock options and warrants. We'll explain this in more detail later, but, like the working capital clause, it can impact the overall value of the deal based on what people are expecting to receive.

Asset Deal versus Stock Deal

While price is usually the first issue on every seller's mind, structure should be second. Lawyers talk about two types of deals, asset deals and stock deals, but there are numerous structural issues surrounding each type of deal. Let's begin by discussing the basics of an asset deal and a stock deal.

In general, all sellers want to do stock deals and all buyers want to do asset deals. Just to increase the confusion level, a stock deal can be done for cash and an asset deal can be done for stock. Don't confuse the type of deal with the actual consideration received.

Sarcastic VCs on the seller side will refer to an asset deal as a situation "when buying a company is not really buying a company." Buyers will request this structure, with the idea that they will buy only the particular assets that they want out of a company, leave certain liabilities (read: "warts") behind, and live happily ever after. If you engage lawyers and accountants in this discussion, they'll ramble on about something regarding taxes, accounting, and liabilities, but our experience is that most of the time the acquirer is just looking to buy the crown jewels, explicitly limit its liabilities, and craft a simpler deal for itself at the expense of the seller. We notice that asset deals are more popular in shaky economic times since acquirers are trying to avoid creditor issues and successor liability. One saw relatively few asset deals in the late 1990s, but in early 2000 asset deals became much more popular; yet by 2012 asset deals are once again rarely seen and only in distressed situations.

While asset deals can work for a seller, the fundamental problem for the seller is that the company hasn't actually been sold! The assets have left the company (and are now owned by the buyer), but there is still a shell corporation with contracts, liabilities, potential employees, and tax forms to file. Even if the company is relatively clean from a corporate hygiene perspective, it may take several years (depending on tax, capital structure, and jurisdictional concerns) to wind down the company. During this time, the officers and directors of the company are still on the hook and the company presumably has few assets to operate the business (since they were sold to the buyer).

In the case of a stock deal, the acquirer is buying the entire company. Once the acquisition is closed, the seller's company disappears into the corporate structure of the buyer and there is nothing left, except possibly some T-shirts that found their way into the hands of spouses and the company sign that used to be on the door just before the deal closed. There is nothing to wind down, and the company is history.

So is an asset deal bad or is it just a hassle? It depends. It can be really bad if the seller has multiple subsidiaries, numerous contracts, employees with severance commitments, or disgruntled shareholders, or it is close to insolvency. In this case, the officers and directors may be taking on fraudulent conveyance liability by consummating an asset deal. It's merely a hassle if the company is in relatively good shape, is very small, or has few shareholders to consider. Of course, if any of these things are true, then the obvious rhetorical question is "Why doesn't the acquirer just buy the whole company via a stock deal?"

In our experience, we see stock deals the vast majority of the time. Often the first draft of the LOI is an asset deal, but it's often the first point raised by sophisticated sellers and they are often successful in ending up with a stock deal except in extreme circumstances when the company is in dire straits. Many buyers go down a path to discuss all the protection they get from an asset deal. This is generally nonsense since a stock deal can be configured to provide functionally equivalent protection for the buyer with a lot less hassle for the seller. In addition, asset deals are no longer the protection they used to be with regard to successor liability in a transaction, since courts are much more eager to find a company that purchases substantial assets of another company to be a so-called successor in interest with respect to liabilities of the seller.

The structure of the deal is also tied closely to the tax issues surrounding a deal. Once you start trying to optimize for structure and taxes, you end up defining the type of consideration (stock or cash) the seller can receive. It can get complicated very quickly, and pretty soon you can feel like you are climbing up a staircase in an Escher drawing. We'll dig into tax and consideration in a bit; just realize that they are all linked together and usually ultimately impact price, which is—after all—what the seller usually cares most about.

The Entrepreneur's Perspective

If your company is in bad shape, you will probably have no choice but to do an asset sale and deal with the liabilities and associated winding down of the entity yourself. You should be prepared for this situation and constantly be calculating the expense and hassle of an asset deal to understand what kind of alternatives you're willing to consider.

Form of Consideration

Imagine the following conversation between an entrepreneur and a VC.

> Entrepreneur: "I just received an offer for the company for $15 million from Company X."
>
> VC: "Awesome. Who's Company X? I've never heard of them."
>
> Entrepreneur: "It's a private company funded by Venture Firm Y."
>
> VC: "Cool—$15 million. Is it a cash deal?"
>
> Entrepreneur: "No, it's all stock."
>
> VC: "Hmmm—are you getting preferred or common stock?"
>
> Entrepreneur: "Common stock. Why?"
>
> VC: "How much money has the company raised?"
>
> Entrepreneur: "$110 million."
>
> VC: "What's the liquidation preference? Is it a participating preferred? What's the valuation of the company?"
>
> Entrepreneur: "Oh, I'm not worried about that stuff. The valuation is $300 million and they say they are going public soon."

If you've paid attention to the first part of this book, you know where this is going. The entrepreneur just received an offer for his company for 5 percent of the acquirer (actually 4.76 percent on a post-transaction basis) in an illiquid stock in a private company that is sitting under $110 million of liquidation preferences that are probably participating. If our friend calls his friendly neighborhood financial appraiser to do a valuation analysis, he'll find out the $15 million he thinks he is getting is actually valued at a lot less (probably good for tax purposes, not so good for buying beer, sports cars, and second houses).

The form of consideration matters a lot. Cash is—well—king. Everything else is something less. And it can be a lot less. Did you hear the one where the acquirer offered "free software products" up to a certain amount in exchange for the company's assets? Gee, er, thanks.

Obviously cash is easy to understand and to value. Stock can be more complicated. If it's stock in a private company, understanding the existing capital structure is a critical first step to understanding what you are getting. If it's stock in a public company, you'll want to ask a variety of questions, including whether the stock is freely tradable, registered, or subject to a lockup agreement. If it's freely tradable, will you be considered an insider after the transaction and have any selling restrictions? If it's not freely tradable, what kind of registration rights will you have? It can get messy quickly, especially if you try to optimize for tax (there's that tax thing again).

It's important to realize that the value of your company and the price you are getting paid may not be the same. Don't let yourself get locked into a price early in the negotiation until you understand the form of consideration you are receiving.

Assumption of Stock Options

After considering price and structure, it is time to discuss other major deal points generally found in an LOI. One item to note here: absence of these terms in your particular LOI may not be a good thing, as in our experience detailed LOIs are better than vague ones (although be careful not to overlawyer the LOI). Specifically, this is the case because during the LOI discussions most of the negotiating is between the business principals of the deal, not their lawyers, who will become the main deal drivers after the signing of the term sheet. Our experience is that leaving material business points to the lawyers will slow down the process, increase deal costs, and cause much unneeded pain and angst. Our suggestion would be to always have most of the key terms clearly spelled out in the LOI and agreed to by the business principals before the lawyers bring out their clubs, quivers, and broadswords.

It is time to discuss the treatment of the stock option plan. The way stock options are handled (regardless of how you address the 409A issues, which we'll discuss later) can vary greatly in the LOI. The first issue to consider is whether the stock option plan is being assumed by the buyer and, if so, whether the assumption of the option plan is being netted against (or subtracted from) the purchase price. In some cases, the buyer will simply assume the option pool in addition to the base consideration being received; however, it's typically the case that if the buyer agrees to assume the option plan, then the aggregate price will be adjusted accordingly, as very few things are actually free in this world.

Let's presume the option pool is not going to be assumed by the buyer. The seller now has several things to consider. Some option plans, especially those that are poorly constructed, don't have any provisions that deal with an acquisition when the plan is not assumed. If the plan is silent, it's conceivable that when the deal closes and the options are not assumed, they will simply disappear. This sucks for anyone holding options and is probably not in the spirit of the original option plan.

Most contemporary option plans have provisions whereby all granted options fully vest immediately prior to an acquisition should the plan and/or options underneath the plan not be assumed by the buyer. While this clearly benefits the option holders and helps incentivize the employees of the seller who hold options, it does have an impact on the seller and the buyer. In the case of the seller, it will effectively allocate a portion of the purchase price to the option holders. In the case of the buyer, it will create a situation in which there is no forward incentive for the employees to stick around since their option value is fully vested and paid at the time of the acquisition, resulting in the buyer having to come up with additional incentive packages to retain employees on a going-forward basis.

Many lawyers will advise in favor of a fully vesting option plan because it forces the buyer to assume the option plan, because if it did not, then the option holders would immediately become shareholders of the combined entities. Under the general notion that fewer shareholders are better, this acceleration provision motivates buyers to assume option plans. This theory holds true only if there is a large number of option holders.

In the past few years we've seen cases where the buyer has used this provision against the seller and its preferred shareholders. In these cases the buyer has explicitly denied assuming the options, wanting the current option holders to become target shareholders immediately prior to the consummation of the merger and thus receive direct consideration in the merger. The result is that merger consideration is shifted away from prior shareholders and allocated to employees whose prior position was that of an unvested option holder. This transfer of consideration shifts away from the prior shareholders—generally preferred stockholders, company management, and former founders—into the pockets of other employees. The buyer acquires a happy employee base upon closing of the merger. This is an option for the buyer only if the employee base of the target is relatively small. In addition, the buyer can grant additional options to the management and employees that it wants to keep going forward so that in the end the only stakeholders worse off are the preferred stockholders, former employees, and former founders of the company.

There are two more critical issues: what happens if the acquisition is in cash versus public stock versus private stock, and who pays for the basis value of the stock options? We're going to ignore tax considerations for the moment (although you shouldn't ignore them in a real-world acquisition). If I'm an employee of a seller, I'm going to value cash differently from public stock (restricted or unrestricted) and public stock options differently from private stock (or options). If the buyer is public or is paying cash, the calculation is pretty straightforward and can be easily explained to the employee. If the buyer is private, this becomes much more challenging and is something that management and the representatives of the seller who are structuring the transaction should think through carefully.

The *basis of stock options* (also known as the *strike price* or *barter element*) reduces the value of the stock options. Specifically, if the value of a share of stock in a transaction is $1 and the basis of the stock option is $0.40, the actual value of the stock option at the time of the transaction is $0.60. Many sellers forget to try to recapture the value of the barter element in the purchase price and allow the total purchase price to be the gross value of the stock options (vested and unvested) rather than getting incremental credit on the purchase price for the barter element.

Let's assume you have a $100 million cash transaction with $10 million going to option holders, 50 percent of which are vested and 50 percent are unvested. Assume for simplicity that the buyer is assuming unvested options but including them in the total purchase price (the $100 million) and that the total barter element of the vested stock is $1 million and the barter element of the unvested stock is $3 million. The vested stock has a value of $4 million ($5 million value minus $1 million barter element) and the unvested stock has a value of $2 million ($5 million value minus $3 million barter element). So, the option holders are going to net only $6 million total. Often the seller will catch the vested stock amount (e.g., vested options will account for $4 million of the $100 million) but the full $5 million will be allocated to the unvested options (instead of the actual value/cost to the buyer of $2 million). This is a material difference (e.g., the difference between $91 million going to the nonoption holders versus $94 million).

Of course, all of this assumes that the stock options are in the money. If the purchase price of the transaction puts the options out of the money (e.g., the purchase price is below the liquidation preference) all of this is irrelevant since the options are worthless.

The Entrepreneur's Perspective

In most cases, your employees got your company to where it is. Do not sell them short in an exit, whether or not there is an earn-out that compels you to keep them happy. Your reputation as an entrepreneur is at stake here, plus you want to do the right thing.

Representations, Warranties, and Indemnification

Every LOI will have some mention of *representations and warranties*, also called "reps and warranties" or just "reps" by those in the know. The reps and warranties are the facts and assurances about the business that one party gives the other. In most LOIs, the language in this paragraph is light in substance, but this section can have a profound effect on the deal and consume a ridiculous amount of legal time during the negotiation of the definitive agreement.

The first thing to note is who is making the representations. Does it say the selling company will be making the reps, or does it say the selling company and its shareholders are on the hook? Or, more typically, is it silent as to who exactly is stepping up to the plate? Given that many shareholders (including VCs and individuals who hold stock in the selling company) are unwilling or unable to represent and warrant to the seller's situation, it's important to resolve in the LOI who is actually making the reps. Optimally you can get this solved before the lawyers start fighting over this, since most buyers will eventually accept that the company, instead of the underlying shareholders in the company, is making the reps.

All LOIs will have something regarding *indemnification* in the event that one of the reps or warranties is breached. Considering how important this provision is to the seller in an acquisition, it's often the case that the buyer will try to sneak past the following language in the LOI.

> The Company shall make standard representations and warranties and provide standard indemnification to Acquirer.

This is code for:

> We are really going to negotiate hard on the indemnification terms, but don't want to tell you at this stage so that you'll sign the LOI and become committed to doing the deal. Really—trust us—our deal guys and lawyers are nice and cuddly.

Depending upon the situation of the seller (perhaps the seller is in a position whereby it wants to get the buyer committed more than vice versa and is willing to take its chances with the lawyers arguing), we'd suggest that you at least sketch out what the indemnification will look like. Again, once the lawyers get involved, arguments like "It's market and it's nonnegotiable" or "I get this on all of my deals" get bantered about endlessly.

The buyer usually makes some reps as well, but since it is paying for the seller, these are typically pretty lightweight unless the buyer is paying in private company stock. If you are a seller and you are getting private stock from the buyer, a completely logical starting point is to make all the reps and warranties reciprocal.

The Entrepreneur's Perspective

As long as most of your reps and warranties are qualified by a phrase like "to the extent currently known...," you should have no problem signing them. Arguing against them is a big red flag to investors or buyers.

Escrow

The escrow is another hotly negotiated term that often is left ambiguous in the LOI. The escrow (also known as a holdback) is money that the buyer is going to hang on to for some period of time to satisfy any issue that comes up postacquisition that is not disclosed in the purchase agreement.

In some LOIs we've seen extensive details—with each provision of the escrow agreement spelled out—including the percentage of the holdbacks, length of time, and carve-outs to the indemnity agreement. In other cases, there is simply a declaration that "standard escrow and indemnity terms shall apply." Since there really isn't any such thing as a standard term, this is another buyer-centric trap for deferring what can become a brutal negotiation in the post-LOI stage. Whatever the escrow arrangement is, it will decrease the actual purchase price should any claim be brought under it, so the terms of the agreement can be very important since they directly impact the value that the seller receives.

In our experience over hundreds of acquisitions, an escrow is typically set up as the sole remedy for breaches of the reps and warranties, with a few exceptions, known as carve-outs. Normally between 10 percent and 20 percent of the aggregate purchase price is set aside for between 12 and 24 months to cure any breaches of the reps. While this is usually where the escrow terms end up (and are usually described as the *escrow caps*), it can take a herculean effort to get there. Buyers often try to overreach, especially if the parameters are not defined in the LOI, by asking for things such as uncapped indemnity if anything goes wrong, personal liability of company executives and major shareholders, and even the ability to capture more value than the deal is worth.

The Entrepreneur's Perspective

Buyers overreaching on the escrow terms are silly, especially if you have a well-run business with audited financials and outside directors. Remember, when a public company gets acquired, its reps and warranties usually expire at the closing!

The carve-outs to the escrow caps typically include fraud, capitalization, and taxes. Occasionally a buyer will press for intellectual property ownership to be carved out. We've also started to see liabilities resulting from lack of 409A compliance be carved out in escrow agreements under the argument that 409A is equivalent to taxes. In all cases, the maximum of the carve-out should be the aggregate deal value, as the seller shouldn't have to come up with more than it was paid in the deal to satisfy an escrow claim.

A lot of buyers will say something like "Well, I can't figure the specifics out until I do more due diligence." We say baloney to that as we've yet to meet a buyer that was unable to put an initial escrow proposal, with some detail and caps defined, in the LOI. This language is still subject to due diligence but is harder to retrade after it has been agreed to since something of substance has to emerge for there to be a legitimate discussion about it.

Finally, the form of consideration of the escrow is important. In a cash deal, it's easy—it's cash. However, in a stock deal or a deal that has a combination of cash and stock, the value of the escrow will float with the stock price, and the value can vary even more dramatically over time if it's private company stock. There are lots of permutations on how to best manage this on the seller side; you should be especially thoughtful about this if you have concerns that the buyer's stock is particularly volatile. Imagine the situation where the stock price declines but the buyer's escrow claims are of greater value than the stock in escrow represents. Reasonable people should be able to agree that the seller doesn't have to come up with extra money to satisfy the claims.

Confidentiality/Nondisclosure Agreement

While VCs will almost never sign nondisclosure agreements (NDAs) in the context of an investment, NDAs are almost always mandatory in an acquisition. If the deal falls apart and ultimately doesn't happen, both parties (the seller and the buyer) are left in a position where they have sensitive information regarding the other. Furthermore, it's typically one of the few legally binding provisions in an LOI other than the location of jurisdiction for any legal issues and breakup fees. If the deal closes, this provision largely becomes irrelevant since the buyer now owns the seller.

Both the buyer and the seller should be aligned in their desire to have a comprehensive and strong confidentiality agreement since both parties benefit. If you are presented with a weak (or one-sided) confidentiality agreement, it could mean that the acquirer is attempting to learn about your company through the due diligence process and may or may not be intent on closing the deal.

Generally a one-sided confidentiality agreement makes no sense—this should be a term that both sides are willing to sign up to with the same standard. Public companies are often very particular about the form of the confidentiality agreement. While we don't recommend sellers sign just anything, if it's bidirectional you are probably in a pretty safe position.

Employee Matters

Although the board of a company has a fiduciary responsibility to all employees and shareholders of a company, it's unfortunately not always the case that management and the board are looking out for all employees and all shareholders in an acquisition. In public company acquisitions you often hear about egregious cases of senior management looking out for themselves (and their board members helping them line their pockets) at the expense of shareholders. This can also happen in acquisitions of private companies, where the buyer knows it needs the senior executives to stick around and is willing to pay something extra for it. Of course, the opposite can happen as well, where the consideration in an acquisition is slim and the investors try to grab all the nickels for themselves, leaving management with little or nothing.

It's important for management and the board to have the proper perspective on their individual circumstances in the context of the specific deal that is occurring. Whenever we are on the board of a company that is a seller, we prefer to defer the detailed discussion about individual compensation until after the LOI is signed and the managements of the buyer and the seller have time to do due diligence on each other, build a working relationship, and understand the logical roles of everyone going forward. Spending too much time up front negotiating management packages often results in a lot of very early deal fatigue, typically makes buyers uncomfortable with the motivation of the management team for the sale, and can often create a huge wedge between management and the other shareholders on the seller's side. We aren't suggesting that management and employees shouldn't be taken care of appropriately in a transaction; rather, we believe there won't be an opportunity to take care of everyone appropriately if you don't actually get to the transaction. Overnegotiating this too early often causes a lot of unnecessary stress, especially between management and their investors.

While we don't recommend negotiating the employment agreements too early in the process, we also don't recommend leaving them to the very end of the process. Many buyers do this so they can exert as much pressure as possible on the key employees of the seller as everyone is ready to get the deal done and the only thing hanging it up is the employment agreements. Ironically, many sellers view the situation exactly the opposite way (i.e., now that the deal is basically done, we can ask for a bunch of extra stuff from the buyer). Neither of these positions is very effective, and both usually result in unnecessary tension at the end of the deal process and occasionally create a real rift between buyer and seller posttransaction.

This is a particular situation where balance is important. When it comes to employee matters, there's nothing wrong with a solid negotiation. Just make sure that it happens in the context of a deal or you may never actually get the deal done.

Conditions to Close

Buyers normally include certain conditions to closing in the LOI. These can be generic phrases such as "Subject to Board approval by Acquirer," "Subject to the Company not having a material adverse change," or "Subject to due diligence and agreement on definitive documents." There can also be phrases that are specific to the situation of the seller such as "Subject to the Company settling outstanding copyright litigation," or "Subject to Company liquidating its foreign subsidiaries." We generally don't get too concerned about this provision, because any of these deal outs are very easy to trigger should the buyer decide that it doesn't want to do the deal.

Instead of worrying about whether the provision is part of the LOI, we tend to focus on the details of the conditions to close since this is another data point about the attitude of the buyer. If the list of conditions is long and complex, you likely have a suitor with very particular tastes. In this case it's worth pushing back early on a few of these conditions to close, especially the more constraining ones, to learn about what your negotiation process is going to be like.

The Entrepreneur's Perspective

Remember, once buyers are in a significant legal and due diligence process with you, they are as emotionally and financially committed to a deal as you are (and in many cases, their reputation is on the line, too).

As the seller, you should expect that once you've agreed to specific conditions to close, you will be held to them. It's worth addressing these early in the due diligence process so you don't get hung up by something unexpected when you have to liquidate a foreign subsidiary or some other bizarre condition to close, especially if you've never done this before.

The No-Shop Clause

Signing a letter of intent starts a serious and expensive process for both the buyer and the seller. As a result, you should expect that a buyer will insist on a no-shop provision similar to the one that we discussed around term sheets. In the case of an acquisition, no-shop provisions are almost always unilateral, especially if you are dealing with an acquisitive buyer.

As the seller you should be able to negotiate the length of time into a reasonable zone such as 45 to 60 days. If the buyer is asking for more than 60 days, you should push back hard since it's never in a seller's interest to be locked up for an extended period of time. In addition, most deals should be able to be closed within 60 days from signing of the LOI, so having a reasonable deadline forces everyone to be focused on the actual goal of closing the deal.

Since most no-shop agreements will be unilateral, the buyer will typically have the right but not the obligation to cancel the no-shop if it decides not to go forward with the deal. As a result, the time window is particularly important since the seller is likely to be tied up for the length of the no-shop even if the deal doesn't proceed. In some cases an honorable buyer who has decided not to move forward with a deal will quickly agree to terminate the no-shop; however, it's more likely that the buyer will simply drag its feet until the no-shop expires.

In cases in which the deal is actively in process and the no-shop period ends, the seller should expect a call from the buyer a few days before the expiration of the no-shop with a request to extend it. There is often some additional leverage that accrues to the seller at this moment in time, including relief from a net worth threshold, potential short-term financing from the buyer, or even very specific concessions around reps and warranties that have been held up in the negotiation. The seller should be careful not to overreach at this moment since the tone for the final phase of the negotiation can be set by the behavior around the extension of the no-shop. If the seller asks for too much at this point in time, it can expect the buyer to tighten down on everything else through the close of the deal.

Rather than fight the no-shop, we've found it more effective to limit the duration of the no-shop period and carve out specific events, most notably financings (at the minimum financings done by the existing syndicate), to keep some pressure on the buyer.

The Entrepreneur's Perspective

As with no-shops with VCs, no-shops with potential buyers should also have an automatic out if the buyer terminates the process.

Fees, Fees, and More Fees

The LOI will usually be explicit about who pays for which costs and what limits exist for the seller to run up transaction costs in the acquisition. Transaction costs associated with an agent or a banker, the legal bill, and any other seller-side costs are typically included in the transaction fee section. Though it's conceivable that the buyer will punt on worrying about who covers transaction fees, most savvy buyers are very focused on making sure the seller ends up eating these, especially if they are meaningful amounts.

Occasionally the concept of a breakup fee comes up for situations where the deal doesn't close or the seller ends up doing a deal with another buyer. Breakup fees are rare in private company VC-backed deals but prevalent in deals where one public company acquires another public company. We generally resist any request of a buyer to institute a breakup fee and tell the potential buyer to rely on the no-shop clause instead. Most buyers of VC-backed companies are much larger and more resource rich than the seller it seeks to acquire, so it strikes us as odd that the buyer would receive a cash windfall if the deal does not close, especially since both parties will have costs incurred in the process. When we are the seller, we rarely ask for a breakup fee.

The Entrepreneur's Perspective

There are some rare circumstances in which a seller can reasonably ask for a breakup fee. If the buyer is competitive and the seller is concerned that the buyer may be entering the process as a fishing expedition as opposed to a good-faith effort to buy the company, or if the seller incurs a massive amount of customer or employee risk by entering into the deal, a breakup fee may be appropriate.

Registration Rights

When a public company is buying a private company for stock, it's important for the seller to understand the registration characteristics and rights associated with the stock it will be receiving. Some buyers will try to ignore this; a good seller should work hard up front to get agreement on what it will be receiving.

Often a buyer will offer unregistered stock with a promise to register the shares. It's important that the seller recognize that this is almost always a nonbinding promise since the buyer can't guarantee when it can register the shares because it is dependent on the Securities and Exchange Commission (SEC) for this and it doesn't control the SEC. The past history of the buyer with the SEC is crucial, including knowing the current status of SEC filings, any outstanding registration statements, and any promises that the buyer has made to shareholders of other companies it has acquired.

We've experienced several cases in which buyers have promised a quick registration only to drag their feet on the filing after the deal or have the filing get hung up at the SEC. In today's regulatory environment, we've been amazed by the poor behavior of several of the big four accounting firms when they state they don't have time to work on acquisition accounting questioned by the SEC, especially in situations in which the accounting firm is not going to be working with the acquirer after the acquisition.

Unregistered stock becomes tradable after a 12-month waiting period, but a year can be a long time and involve a lot of volatility, especially in a thinly traded stock. Make sure you are getting what you think you are getting.

Shareholder Representatives

Acquisitions are not actually finished when the deal closes and the money trades hands. There are terms such as managing the escrow, dealing with earn-outs, working capital adjustments, and even litigation concerning reps and warranties that will last long into the future. In every acquisition, there is someone—referred to as the shareholder representative—who is appointed to be the representative of all the former shareholders in the seller to deal with these issues.

This lucky person, who is generally not paid anything for his services, gets to deal with all the issues that arise between the buyer and the seller after the transaction. These issues can be based around buyer's remorse or be legitimate issues, but are often time-consuming, are expensive to deal with, and impact the ultimate financial outcome of the deal.

Traditionally either an executive from the seller or one of the VC board members takes on this role. If nothing ever comes up, it's a complete nonevent for this person. However, when something goes awry where the buyer makes a claim on the escrow or threatens to sue the former shareholders of the company, this job often becomes a giant time-wasting nightmare. The shareholder rep, who typically has a full-time job, limited money from the deal (often tied up in the escrow) to hire professionals to help him, and usually isn't a subject matter expert in anything that is at issue, ends up being responsible for dealing with it. If it's an executive of the seller, he might still be working for the buyer. In any case, this person is now making decisions that impact all of the shareholders and subsequently ends up spending time and energy communicating with them. Finally, some buyers, in an effort to exert even more pressure on the system, sue the shareholder rep directly.

We've each been shareholder reps many times. Several years ago, we decided never to be shareholder reps again, as we see no upside in taking on this responsibility.

If you somehow end up being the shareholder rep, make sure you negotiate a pool of money into the merger agreement that you can dip into to hire professionals to support you should something arise that you have to deal with. We often see a separate escrow that is used exclusively to pay for the expenses of the shareholder representative. If nothing else, this works to be a good shield to a bad-acting buyer since it will see that you have money to hire lawyers to yell at its lawyers.

Never ask someone who will be working for the buyer posttransaction to be the shareholder rep. If you do this, you are asking this person to get into a winner-takes-all fight against his current employer, and that is not a happy position for anyone to be in. The only time this ever works is if the shareholder rep has a role that is critical to the buyer where the threat of the rep quitting will help influence the outcome in a way positive to the seller. Regardless, this is a stressful and uncomfortable position to be in.

You should also be wary of letting a VC take on this role. Escrow and litigation dynamics are time sensitive, and we've had experiences where other VCs involved as the shareholder rep paid little or no attention to their responsibilities since they didn't fully understand or appreciate the legal dynamics surrounding their role. We've had some bizarre experiences, including a shareholder rep who was a VC (a co-investor in a deal with us) who blew an escrow situation by ignoring the notice he received from the buyer that a claim had been breached. The notice period was 30 days, and 31 days after receiving the notice, the VC received another letter saying the escrow had been deducted by the amount of the claim. Fortunately we had a good relationship with the lawyer on the side of the buyer and were able to get an exception made, but the buyer had no obligation to do this other than as a result of goodwill that existed between the parties.

As a result of our experience with this over the years, Jason co-founded a company called Shareholder Representative Services (SRS—www.shareholderrep.com) that is an organization that acts as a shareholder rep. The cost, relative to the overall value of the deal, of using a firm like SRS is modest and you get professionals who spend 100 percent of their time playing the role of shareholder rep. When there is litigation, they get sued and deal with all of the details. Given the wide range of deals they've worked on as shareholder reps, they tend to have wide-ranging and extensive experience with both buyers and their lawyers.

Legal Things Every Entrepreneur Should Know

There are a few legal issues that we've seen consistently become hurdles for entrepreneurs and their lawyers. While in some cases they will simply be a hassle to clean up in a financing or an exit, they often have meaningful financial implications for the company and, in the worst case, can seriously damage the value of your business. We aren't your lawyers or giving you legal advice here (our lawyers made us write that), but we encourage you to understand these issues rather than just assume that your lawyer got them right.

Intellectual Property

Intellectual property (IP) issues can kill a startup before you even really begin. Following is an example.

You and a friend go out and get some beers. You start telling him about your new company that will revolutionize X and make you a lot of money. You spend several hours talking about the business model, what you need to build, and the product requirements. After one beer too many, you both stumble home happy.

Your friend goes back to work at his job at Company X-like. You picked this particular friend to vet your idea because you know that your company is similar to some cutting-edge work he does at X-like. There is even a chance that you'd want to hire this friend one day.

You spend the next six months bootstrapping your company and release a first version of your product. A popular tech blog writes about it and you start getting inbound calls from VCs wanting to fund you. You can't stop smiling and are excited about how glorious life as an entrepreneur is.

The next day your beer buddy calls and says that he's been laid off from Company X-like and wants to join your company. You tell him as soon as you get funding you'd love to hire him. Your friend says, "That's okay—I can start today for no pay since I own 50 percent of the company." You sit in stunned silence for a few seconds.

As you discuss the issue, your friend tells you that he owns 50 percent of the IP of your company since you guys went out and basically formed the company over beers. You tell him that you disagree and he doesn't own any of the company. He tells you his uncle is a lawyer.

As strange as this sounds, this is a real example. While we think the claim by your so-called friend is ridiculous, if he takes action (via his uncle, who is likely working for him for free) he can slow down your VC financing. If he stays after you and you don't give him something, it's possible that he'll end up completely stifling your chance to raise money. If you happen to get lucky (for instance, if your so-called friend accidentally gets hit by a bus), you still have the outstanding issue that Company X-like may also have a claim on the IP if there is an actual lawsuit filed and X-like happens to stumble upon piecing the story together.

There are endless stories like this in startup land, including the history of the founding of Facebook popularized (and fictionalized) by the movie *The Social Network*. Our example is one extreme, but there are others, like students starting a company in an MBA class where two go on to actually start the business while the other two don't, but terrorize the company for ownership rights later due to their claimed IP contributions. Or the entrepreneur who hired a contractor to write code for him, paid the contractor, but still ended up in litigation with the contractor who claimed he owned IP above and beyond what he was paid for.

When things like this come up, even the most battle-hardened VC will pause and make sure that there are no real IP issues involved. Responsible VCs who want to invest in your company will work with you to solve this stuff, especially when absurd claims like the examples we just gave are being made. In our experience, there's often a straightforward resolution except in extreme circumstances.

The key is being careful, diligent, and reasonably paranoid up front. When friends are involved, you can usually work this stuff out with a simple conversation. However, when talking to random people, be careful of unscrupulous characters, especially those you know nothing about.

Some entrepreneurs, and many lawyers, think the right solution is to carefully guard your idea or have everyone you talk to sign a nondisclosure agreement. We don't agree with this position. Instead, we encourage entrepreneurs to be very open with their ideas, and we generally believe NDAs aren't worth very much. However, be conscious of whom you are talking to and, if you start heading down the path of actually creating a business, make sure you have competent legal counsel help you document it.

Employment Issues

The most common lawsuits entrepreneurs are on the receiving end of are ones around employment issues. These are never pleasant, especially in the context of an employee you've recently fired, but they are an unfortunate result of today's work context.

There are a few things you can do to protect against this. First, make sure that everyone you hire is an *at-will employee*. Without these specific words in the offer letter, you can end up dealing with state employment laws (which vary from state to state) that determine whether you can fire someone. We've encountered some challenging situations in states that made firing people in the United States almost as challenging as firing them in France.

Next, consider whether you want to prebake severance terms into an offer letter. For instance, you might decide that if you let someone go, they will receive additional vesting or cash compensation. If you don't decide this at the outset, you may be left with a situation where you are able to fire someone, but they claim that you owe them something on the way out. On the other hand, determining up-front severance is about as much fun as negotiating a prenuptial agreement, and the downside to it is that it limits your flexibility, especially if the company is in a difficult financial situation and needs to fire people to lower its burn rate in order to conserve cash to survive.

Every entrepreneur should know at least one good employment lawyer. Dealing with these particular issues can be stressful and unpredictable, especially given the extensive rules around discrimination that again vary from state to state, and a knowledgeable employment lawyer can quickly help you get to an appropriate resolution when something comes up.

State of Incorporation

While you can incorporate your business in 50 states, there are a few preferred states to incorporate in, especially when you are planning to seek VC backing. Most VCs prefer one of three states: Delaware, whichever state the company is in, or whichever state the VC is located in.

Delaware is common because corporate law for Delaware is well defined and generally business friendly, and most lawyers in the United States are adept at dealing with Delaware law. If you are planning on ultimately having an initial public offering (IPO), most investment bankers will insist on you being incorporated in Delaware before they will take you public. More important, lots of obvious things that are difficult or not permitted in some states, such as faxed signature pages or rapid response to requests for changes in corporate documents, are standard activities in Delaware.

The only two disadvantages of being incorporated in Delaware are that you will have to pay some extra (but very modest) taxes and potentially comply with two sets of corporate laws. For instance, if you are located in California and are a Delaware corporation, you'll have to comply with Delaware law and some of California law, too, despite being a Delaware corporation.

Either of the other two common choices, the location of the company or the location of the VC, is generally fine also. However, if a VC has no experience with your state's corporate laws, you'll occasionally find resistance for incorporating in your state. We view this as rational behavior on the part of the VC, especially when the VC joins the board because the VC then ends up being personally liable as a director under the state's corporate laws. Since these laws can vary widely, we always encourage Delaware as the default case.

Accredited Investors

Though this isn't a book about securities laws (which, if it were, would make it a dreadfully dull book), much of it is actually about selling securities to investors. There are lots of laws that you need to comply with in order to not get in trouble with the SEC, and thus that is one of the major reasons that you need to have a good lawyer.

Most of the issues can be avoided by following one piece of advice. Do not ask your hairdresser, auto mechanic, and bag boy at the grocery store to buy stock in your company unless they are independently wealthy. There are laws that effectively say that only rich and sophisticated people are *accredited investors* allowed to buy stock in private companies. If you try to raise money from people who do not fit this definition, then you've probably committed a securities violation. Normally, the SEC doesn't catch most people who do this, but it does happen sometimes.

If you ignore this advice and sell stock in your private company to people who don't fit the SEC's definition of an accredited investor, then you have a lifelong problem on your hands. Specifically, these nonaccredited investors can force you to buy back their shares for at least their purchase price anytime they want, despite how your company is doing. This *right of rescission* is a very real thing that we see from time to time. It is particularly embarrassing when the person forcing the buyback is a close family friend or relative who should not have been offered the stock in the first place.

Filing an 83(b) Election

This is another "if you don't do it right in the beginning you can't fix it later" issue. The punch line of not filing an 83(b) election within 30 days after receiving your stock in a company will almost always result in you losing capital gains treatment of your stock when you sell it. We refer to this as the mistake that will cause you to pay three times the amount of taxes that you should pay.

The 83(b) election is a simple form that takes two minutes to execute. Most lawyers will provide the standard form as part of granting your stock. Some will even provide a stamped and addressed envelope, and the most client-friendly lawyers will even mail the form for you. Or you can just Google "83(b) election" and download the form yourself. Note that you must send the form to the appropriate IRS service center.

We've had firsthand experience with this and it's a bummer when you are in the middle of an acquisition and you realize the 83(b) election is unsigned under a pile of papers on your desk. For a firsthand account of this, take a look at the chapter titled "To 83(b) or Not to 83(b)" in Brad's and David Cohen's book *Do More Faster* (John Wiley & Sons, 2010).

Section 409A Valuations

Our last random legal topic that often rears its ugly head around an acquisition is Section 409A of the tax code, also known as the 409A valuation. Section 409A says that all stock options given to employees of a company need to be at *fair market value*.

In the old days before the turn of the millennium (pre-409A), the board of a private company could determine what the fair market value of a share of common stock was and this was acceptable to the IRS. It became common practice that the share price for the common stock, which is also the *exercise* price for the stock options being granted, was typically valued at 10 percent of the price of the last round of preferred stock. The exception was when a company was within 18 months of an IPO, in which case the price of the common stock converged with the price of the preferred stock as the IPO drew nearer.

For some reason the IRS decided this wasn't the right way to determine fair market value, came up with a new approach in Section 409A of the tax code, and created dramatic penalties for the incorrect valuation of stock options. The penalties included excise taxes on the employee and potential company penalties. In addition, some states, such as California, instituted their own penalties at the state level. When Section 409A was first drafted, it sounded like a nightmare.

However, the IRS gave everyone a way out, also known throughout the legal industry as a *safe harbor*. If a company used a professional valuation firm, the valuation would be assumed to be correct unless the IRS could prove otherwise, which is not an easy thing to do. In contrast, if the company chose not to use a professional valuation firm, then the company would have to prove the valuation was correct, which is also a hard thing to do.

The predictable end result of this was the creation of an entirely new line of business for accountants and a bunch of new valuation firms. Section 409A effectively created new overhead for doing business that helped support the accounting profession. Although we have a bunch of friends who work for 409A valuation firms, we don't believe that any of this is additive in any way to the company or to the value-creation process. While the costs are not steep, the $5,000 to $15,000 per year that a typical private company will pay for 409A valuations could easily be spent on something more useful to the company, such as beer or search engine marketing.

An unfortunate side effect is that the 10 percent rule, where common stock was typically valued at 10 percent of the preferred stock, is no longer valid. We often see 409A valuations in early stage companies valuing common stock at 20 percent to 30 percent of the preferred stock. As a result, employees make less money in a liquidity event, as options are more expensive to purchase since their basis (or exercise price) is higher.

Ironically, the IRS also collects fewer taxes, as it receives tax only on the value of the gain (sale price of the stock minus the exercise price). In this case, the accountants are the only financial winners.

Authors' Note

Over the course of this book, we've tried to expose you to all of the issues you'll face during a VC financing. In addition to the nuts and bolts of the term sheet, we've covered the participants in the process, discussed how the fund-raising process works, talked about how VC firms operate, and described some basic negotiating principles. We've also covered a bunch of dos and don'ts around the fund-raising process and, as a bonus, added a chapter deconstructing a typical letter of intent that you'd receive at the beginning of the acquisition process.

Though we are early stage investors, we've tried to explain issues that you'll face in any round of financing. We've tried to be balanced between the entrepreneur's view and the VC's view, as we've been both (although we've now been VCs for much longer). We've also included an entrepreneur's perspective—from Matt Blumberg, the CEO of Return Path—throughout the book.

We know much of this material is dry, and we tried hard to spice it up with our own special brand of humor. We've reviewed it many times but know there are likely some mistakes, as is inevitable with something this complex and subjective. We learn the most from our mistakes and encourage you to email us at jason@foundrygroup.com or brad@foundrygroup.com with anything you find that is unclear or that you believe is incorrect.

Of course, none of the information in this book should be construed as legal advice from us. We are not your lawyers—just a pair of guys who wrote a book that hopefully is helpful to you. If you have legal questions, ask your lawyers. Yes, our lawyers made us write this.

We hope this book has been helpful to you as you work to create an amazing new company.

Appendix A: Sample Term Sheet*

ACME VENTURE CAPITAL 2011, L.P.
Summary of Terms for Proposed Private Placement
of Series A Preferred Stock of
NEWCO.COM
_____, 20__
(Valid for acceptance until _____, 20__)

Issuer: NEWCO.COM (the "Company")

Investor(s): Acme Venture Capital 2011, L.P. and its affiliated partnerships ("Acme") **[and others, if applicable]** ("Investors").

Amount of Financing: An aggregate of $__ million, **[(including $__ from the conversion of outstanding bridge notes)]** representing a __% ownership position on a fully diluted basis, including shares reserved for any employee option pool. **[The individual investment amounts for each Investor are as follows:**

Acme	$_____
Other investor 1	$_____
Other investor 2	$_____
Total:	$_____]

[If there is to be a second closing, differentiate the investors and amounts by each closing.]

Price: $_____ per share (the "Original Purchase Price"). The Original Purchase Price represents a fully diluted premoney valuation of $__ million and a fully diluted postmoney

*Also see AsktheVC.com for more examples.

valuation of $__ million. [**A capitalization table showing the Company's capital structure immediately following the Closing is attached.**] For purposes of the above calculation and any other reference to "fully diluted" in this term sheet, "fully diluted" assumes the conversion of all outstanding preferred stock of the Company, the exercise of all authorized and currently existing stock options and warrants of the Company, and the increase of the Company's existing option pool by [   ] shares prior to this financing.

Post-Closing Capitalization Table

	Shares	Percentage
Common Stock Outstanding		
Employee Stock Options:		
Reserved Pool		
Series A Preferred Outstanding:		
Acme		
[Other Investors]		
Fully Diluted Shares		

Type of Security:

Series A Convertible Preferred Stock (the "Series A Preferred"), initially convertible on a 1:1 basis into shares of the Company's Common Stock (the "Common Stock").

Closing:

Sale of the Series A Preferred (the "Closing") is anticipated to take place _____, 20__.

TERMS OF SERIES A PREFERRED STOCK

Dividends:

The holders of the Series A Preferred shall be entitled to receive noncumulative dividends in preference to any dividend on the Common Stock at the rate of [6%–10%] of the Original Purchase Price per annum [**when and as declared by the Board of Directors**]. The holders of Series A Preferred also shall be entitled to participate pro rata in any dividends paid on the Common Stock on an as-if-converted basis. [*Adding the second bolded section means discretionary dividends, otherwise automatic.*]

Liquidation Preference: In the event of any liquidation or winding up of the Company, the holders of the Series A Preferred shall be entitled to receive in preference to the holders of the Common Stock a per share amount equal to [**2x**] the Original Purchase Price plus any declared but unpaid dividends (the "Liquidation Preference").

[*Choose one of the following three options:*]

[*Option 1: Add this paragraph if you want fully participating preferred:* **After the payment of the Liquidation Preference to the holders of the Series A Preferred, the remaining assets shall be distributed ratably to the holders of the Common Stock and the Series A Preferred on a common equivalent basis.**]

[*Option 2: Add this paragraph if you want participating preferred:* **After the payment of the Liquidation Preference to the holders of the Series A Preferred, the remaining assets shall be distributed ratably to the holders of the Common Stock and the Series A Preferred on a common equivalent basis; provided that the holders of Series A Preferred will stop participating once they have received a total liquidation amount per share equal to [two to five] times the Original Purchase Price, plus any declared but unpaid dividends. Thereafter, the remaining assets shall be distributed ratably to the holders of the Common Stock.**]

[*Option 3: Add this paragraph if you want nonparticipating preferred:* **After the payment of the Liquidation Preference to the holders of the Series A Preferred, the remaining assets shall be distributed ratably to the holders of the Common Stock.**]

Don't use if stock we are buying is fully participating. **[Upon any liquidation or deemed liquidation, holder of the Series A Preferred shall be entitled to receive the greater of (i) the amount they would have received pursuant to the prior sentence, or (ii) the amount they would have received in the event of conversion of the Series A Preferred to Common Stock, in each case taking into account any carve-outs, escrows, or other delayed or contingent payments.]**

A merger, acquisition, sale of voting control, or sale of substantially all of the assets of the Company in which the shareholders of the Company do not own a majority of the outstanding shares of the surviving corporation shall be deemed to be a liquidation.

Conversion:

The holders of the Series A Preferred shall have the right to convert the Series A Preferred, at any time, into shares of Common Stock. The initial conversion rate shall be 1:1, subject to adjustment as provided below.

Automatic Conversion:

All of the Series A Preferred shall be automatically converted into Common Stock, at the then applicable conversion price, upon the closing of a firmly underwritten public offering of shares of Common Stock of the Company at a per share price not less than **[three to five]** times the Original Purchase Price (as adjusted for stock splits, dividends, and the like) per share and for a total offering of not less than **[$15]** million (before deduction of underwriters' commissions and expenses) (a "Qualified IPO"). All, or a portion of each share, of the Series A Preferred shall be automatically converted into Common Stock, at the then applicable conversion price in the event that the holders of at least a majority of the outstanding Series A Preferred consent to such conversion.

Antidilution Provisions: The conversion price of the Series A Preferred will be subject to a [full ratchet/weighted average] adjustment to reduce dilution in the event that the Company issues additional equity securities (other than shares (i) reserved as employee shares described under "Employee Pool" below; (ii) shares issued for consideration other than cash pursuant to a merger, consolidation, acquisition, or similar business combination approved by the Board; (iii) shares issued pursuant to any equipment loan or leasing arrangement, real property leasing arrangement, or debt financing from a bank or similar financial institution approved by the Board; and (iv) shares with respect to which the holders of a majority of the outstanding Series A Preferred waive their antidilution rights) at a purchase price less than the applicable conversion price. In the event of an issuance of stock involving tranches or other multiple closings, the antidilution adjustment shall be calculated as if all stock was issued at the first closing. The conversion price will [also] be subject to proportional adjustment for stock splits, stock dividends, combinations, recapitalizations, and the like.

[Redemption at Option of Investors: **At the election of the holders of at least majority of the Series A Preferred, the Company shall redeem the outstanding Series A Preferred in three annual installments beginning on the [fifth] anniversary of the Closing. Such redemptions shall be at a purchase price equal to the Original Purchase Price plus declared and unpaid dividends.]**

Voting Rights: The Series A Preferred will vote together with the Common Stock and not as a separate class except as specifically provided herein or as otherwise required by law. The Common Stock may be increased or decreased by the vote of holders of a majority of the Common Stock and Series A Preferred voting together on an as-if-converted basis, and without a separate class vote. Each share of Series A Preferred shall have a number of votes equal to the number of shares of Common Stock then issuable upon conversion of such share of Series A Preferred.

Board of Directors: The size of the Company's Board of Directors shall be set at [_____]. The Board shall initially be comprised of _____, as the Acme representative[s] _____, _____, and _____.

At each meeting for the election of directors, the holders of the Series A Preferred, voting as a separate class, shall be entitled to elect **[one]** member[s] of the Company's Board of Directors, which director shall be designated by Acme; the holders of Common Stock, voting as a separate class, shall be entitled to elect **[one]** member[s]; and the remaining directors will be

[Option 1 (if Acme to control more than 50 percent of the capital stock): **mutually agreed upon by the Common and Preferred, voting together as a single class]** *[or Option 2 (if Acme controls less than 50 percent):* **chosen by the mutual consent of the Board of Directors].** *Please note that you may want to make one of the Common seats the person then serving as the CEO.*

[Add this provision if Acme is to get an observer on the Board: **Acme shall have the right to appoint a representative to observe all meetings of the Board of Directors in a nonvoting capacity.]**

The Company shall reimburse expenses of the Series A Preferred directors **[observers]** and advisers for costs incurred in attending meetings of the Board of Directors and other meetings or events attended on behalf of the Company.

Protective Provisions: For so long as any shares of Series A Preferred remain outstanding, consent of the holders of at least a majority of the Series A Preferred shall be required for any action, whether directly or through any merger, recapitalization, or similar event, that (i) alters or changes the rights, preferences, or privileges of the Series A Preferred; (ii) increases or decreases the authorized number of shares of Common or Preferred Stock; (iii) creates (by reclassification or otherwise) any new class or series of shares having rights, preferences, or privileges senior to or on a parity with the Series A Preferred; (iv) results in the redemption or repurchase of any shares of Common Stock (other than pursuant to equity incentive agreements with service providers giving the Company the right to repurchase shares upon the termination of services); (v) results in any merger, other corporate reorganization, sale of control, or any transaction in which all or substantially all of the assets of the Company are sold; (vi) amends or waives any provision of the Company's Certificate of Incorporation or Bylaws; (vii) increases or decreases the authorized size of the Company's Board of Directors; [or] (viii) results in the payment or declaration of any dividend on any shares of Common or Preferred Stock [or (ix) issuance of debt in excess of ($100,000)].

Pay-to-Play:

[*Version 1:* In the event of a Qualified Financing (as defined below), shares of Series A Preferred held by any Investor which is offered the right to participate but does not participate fully in such financing by purchasing at least its pro rata portion as calculated above under "Right of First Refusal" below will be converted into Common Stock.]

[*Version 2:* If any holder of Series A Preferred Stock fails to participate in the next Qualified Financing (as defined below), on a pro rata basis (according to its total equity ownership immediately before such financing) of their Series A Preferred investment, then such holder will have the Series A Preferred Stock it owns converted into Common Stock of the Company. If such holder participates in the next Qualified Financing but not to the full extent of its pro rata share, then only a percentage of its Series A Preferred Stock will be converted into Common Stock (under the same terms as in the preceding sentence), with such percentage being equal to the percent of its pro rata contribution that it failed to contribute.]

A Qualified Financing is the next round of financing after the Series A financing by the Company that is approved by the Board of Directors who determine in good faith that such portion must be purchased pro rata among the stockholders of the Company subject to this provision. Such determination will be made regardless of whether the price is higher or lower than any series of Preferred Stock.

When determining the number of shares held by an Investor or whether this "Pay-to-Play" provision has been satisfied, all shares held by or purchased in the Qualified Financing by affiliated investment funds shall be aggregated. An Investor shall be entitled to assign its rights to participate in this financing and future financings to its affiliated funds and to investors in the Investor and/or its affiliated funds, including funds which are not current stockholders of the Company.]

Information Rights: So long as an Investor continues to hold shares of Series A Preferred or Common Stock issued upon conversion of the Series A Preferred, the Company shall deliver to the Investor the Company's annual budget, as well as audited annual and unaudited quarterly financial statements. Furthermore, as soon as reasonably possible, the Company shall furnish a report to each Investor comparing each annual budget to such financial statements. Each Investor shall also be entitled to standard

| | inspection and visitation rights. These provisions shall terminate upon a Qualified IPO. |
| Registration Rights: | Demand Rights: If Investors holding more than 50 percent of the outstanding shares of Series A Preferred, including Common Stock issued on conversion of Series A Preferred ("Registrable Securities"), or a lesser percentage if the anticipated aggregate offering price to the public is not less than $5,000,000, request that the Company file a Registration Statement, the Company will use its best efforts to cause such shares to be registered; provided, however, that the Company shall not be obligated to effect any such registration prior to the [third] anniversary of the Closing. The Company shall have the right to delay such registration under certain circumstances for one period not in excess of ninety (90) days in any twelve (12) month period. |

The Company shall not be obligated to effect more than two (2) registrations under these demand right provisions, and shall not be obligated to effect a registration (i) during the one hundred eighty (180) day period commencing with the date of the Company's initial public offering, or (ii) if it delivers notice to the holders of the Registrable Securities within thirty (30) days of any registration request of its intent to file a registration statement for such initial public offering within ninety (90) days.

Company Registration: The Investors shall be entitled to "piggyback" registration rights on all registrations of the Company or on any demand registrations of any other investor subject to the right, however, of the Company and its underwriters to reduce the number of shares proposed to be registered pro rata in view of market conditions. If the Investors are so limited, however, no party shall sell shares in such registration other than the Company or the Investor, if any, invoking the demand registration. Unless the registration is with respect to the Company's initial public offering, in no event shall the shares to be sold by the Investors be reduced below 30 percent of the total amount of securities included in the registration. No shareholder of the Company shall be granted piggyback registration rights which would reduce the number of shares includable by the holders of the Registrable Securities in such registration without the consent of the holders of at least a majority of the Registrable Securities.

S-3 Rights: Investors shall be entitled to unlimited demand registrations on Form S-3 (if available to the Company) so long as such registered offerings are not less than $1,000,000.

Expenses: The Company shall bear registration expenses (exclusive of underwriting discounts and commissions) of all such demands, piggybacks, and S-3 registrations (including the expense of one special counsel of the selling shareholders not to exceed $25,000).

Transfer of Rights: The registration rights may be transferred to (i) any partner, member, or retired partner or member or affiliated fund of any holder which is a partnership; (ii) any member or former member of any holder which is a limited liability company; (iii) any family member or trust for the benefit of any individual holder; or (iv) any transferee which satisfies the criteria to be a Major Investor (as defined below); provided the Company is given written notice thereof.

Lockup Provision: Each Investor agrees that it will not sell its shares for a period to be specified by the managing underwriter (but not to exceed 180 days) following the effective date of the Company's initial public offering; provided that all officers, directors, and other 1 percent shareholders are similarly bound. Such lockup agreement shall provide that any discretionary waiver or termination of the restrictions of such agreements by the Company or representatives of underwriters shall apply to Major Investors, pro rata, based on the number of shares held.

Other Provisions: Other provisions shall be contained in the Investor Rights Agreement with respect to registration rights as are reasonable, including cross-indemnification, the period of time in which the Registration Statement shall be kept effective, and underwriting arrangements. The Company shall not require the opinion of Investor's counsel before authorizing the transfer of stock or the removal of Rule 144 legends for routine sales under Rule 144 or for distribution to partners or members of Investors.

Right of First Refusal: Investors who purchase at least _____
                           (____) shares of Series A Preferred

(a "Major Investor") shall have the right in the event the Company proposes to offer equity securities to any person (other than the shares (i) reserved as employee shares described under "Employee Pool" below; (ii) shares issued for consideration other than cash pursuant to a merger, consolidation, acquisition, or similar business combination approved by the Board; (iii) shares issued pursuant to any equipment loan or leasing arrangement, real property leasing arrangement, or debt financing from a bank or similar financial institution approved by the Board; and (iv) shares with respect to which the holders of a majority of the outstanding Series A Preferred waive their right of first refusal) to purchase **[2 times]** their pro rata portion of such shares. Any securities not subscribed for by an eligible Investor may be reallocated among the other eligible Investors. Such right of first refusal will terminate upon a Qualified IPO. For purposes of this right of first refusal, an Investor's pro rata right shall be equal to the ratio of (a) the number of shares of common stock (including all shares of common stock issuable or issued upon the conversion of convertible securities and assuming the exercise of all outstanding warrants and options) held by such Investor immediately prior to the issuance of such equity securities to (b) the total number of shares of common stock outstanding (including all shares of common stock issuable or issued upon the conversion of convertible securities and assuming the exercise of all outstanding warrants and options) immediately prior to the issuance of such equity securities.

Purchase Agreement: The investment shall be made pursuant to a Stock Purchase Agreement reasonably acceptable to the Company and the Investors, which agreement shall contain, among other things, appropriate representations and warranties of the Company, covenants of the Company reflecting the provisions set forth herein, and appropriate conditions of closing, including a management rights letter and an opinion of counsel for the Company.

EMPLOYEE MATTERS

Employee Pool: Prior to the Closing, the Company will reserve shares of its Common Stock so that ___ percent of its fully diluted capital stock following the issuance of its Series A Preferred is available for future issuances to directors, officers, employees, and consultants. The term "Employee Pool" shall include both shares reserved for issuance as stated above, as well as current options outstanding, which aggregate amount is approximately ___ percent of the Company's fully diluted capital stock following the issuance of its Series A Preferred.

Stock Vesting: All stock and stock equivalents issued after the Closing to employees, directors, consultants, and other service providers will be subject to vesting provisions below unless different vesting is approved by the **[unanimous/majority (including the director designated by Acme)** *or* **(including at least one director designated by the Investors)]** consent of the Board of Directors (the "Required Approval"): 25 percent to vest at the end of the first year following such issuance, with the remaining 75 percent to vest monthly over the next three years. The repurchase option shall provide that upon termination of the employment of the shareholder, with or without cause, the Company or its assignee (to the extent permissible under applicable securities law qualification) retains the option to repurchase at the lower of cost or the current fair market value any unvested shares held by such shareholder. Any issuance of shares in excess of the Employee Pool not approved by the Required Approval will be a dilutive event requiring adjustment of the conversion price as provided above and will be subject to the Investors' first offer rights.

The outstanding Common Stock currently held by _____ and _____ (the "Founders") will be subject to similar vesting terms **[provided that the Founders shall be credited with (*one year*) of vesting as of the Closing, with their remaining unvested shares to vest monthly over three years]**.

In the event of a merger, consolidation, sale of assets, or other change of control of the Company and should **[a Founder] [or an Employee]** be terminated without cause within one year after such event, such person shall be entitled to **[one year]** of additional vesting. Other than the foregoing, there shall be no accelerated vesting in any event.

Restrictions on Sales: The Company's Bylaws shall contain a right of first refusal on all transfers of Common Stock, subject to normal exceptions. If the Company elects not to exercise its right, the Company shall assign its right to the Investors.

Proprietary Information and Inventions Agreement:	Each current and former officer, employee, and consultant of the Company shall enter into an acceptable proprietary information and inventions agreement.
[Drag-Along Agreement:	**The holders of the (Founders/Common Stock) Series A Preferred shall enter into a drag-along agreement whereby if a majority of the holders of Series A Preferred agree to a sale or liquidation of the Company, the holders of the remaining Series A Preferred (and Common Stock) shall consent to and raise no objections to such sale.]**
Co-Sale Agreement:	The shares of the Company's securities held by the Founders shall be made subject to a co-sale agreement (with certain reasonable exceptions) with the Investors such that the Founders may not sell, transfer, or exchange their stock unless each Investor has an opportunity to participate in the sale on a pro rata basis. This right of co-sale shall not apply to and shall terminate upon a Qualified IPO.
[Founders' Activities:	**Each of the Founders shall devote 100 percent of his professional time to the Company. Any other professional activities will require the approval of the Board of Directors. Additionally, when a Founder leaves the Company, such Founder shall agree to vote his Common Stock or Series A Preferred (or Common Stock acquired on conversion of Series A or Former Series A Preferred) in the same proportion as all other shares are voted in any vote.]**
[Optional Section]	
[Key Man Insurance:	**The Company shall procure key man life insurance policies for each of the Founders in the amount of ($3,000,000), naming the Company as beneficiary.]**

[*Optional Section*]

[Executive Search: **The Company will use its best efforts to hire a (CEO/CFO/CTO) acceptable to the Investors as soon as practicable following the Closing.**]

OTHER MATTERS

[Initial Public Offering Shares Purchase: **In the event that the Company shall consummate a Qualified IPO, the Company shall use its best efforts to cause the managing underwriter or underwriters of such IPO to offer to Acme the right to purchase at least (5%) of any shares issued under a "friends and family" or "directed shares" program in connection with such Qualified IPO. Notwithstanding the foregoing, all action taken pursuant to this Section shall be made in accordance with all federal and state securities laws, including, without limitation, Rule 134 of the Securities Act of 1933, as amended, and all applicable rules and regulations promulgated by the National Association of Securities Dealers, Inc. and other such self-regulating organizations.**]

No-Shop Agreement: The Company agrees to work in good faith expeditiously toward a closing. The Company and the Founders agree that they will not, directly or indirectly, (i) take any action to solicit, initiate, encourage, or assist the submission of any proposal, negotiation, or offer from any person or entity other than the Investors relating to the sale or issuance of any of the capital stock of the Company or the acquisition, sale, lease, license, or other disposition of the Company or any material part of the stock or assets of the Company, or (ii) enter into any discussions or negotiations, or execute any agreement related to any of the foregoing, and shall notify the Investors promptly of any inquiries by any third parties in regard to the foregoing. Should both parties agree that definitive documents shall not be executed pursuant to this term sheet, then the Company shall have no further obligations under this section.

Capitalization/
Fact Sheet:

The Company shall provide prior to the Closing an updated, post-closing capitalization chart and a list of corporate officers with both business and personal contact information.

Indemnification:

The bylaws and/or other charter documents of the Company shall limit board members' liability and exposure to damages to the broadest extent permitted by applicable law.

[Insurance:

The Company will use its best efforts to obtain directors' and officers' insurance acceptable to Investors as soon as practicable after the Closing.]

Right to Conduct
Activities:

The Company and each Investor hereby acknowledge that some or all of the Investors are professional investment funds, and as such invest in numerous portfolio companies, some of which may be competitive with the Company's business. No Investor shall be liable to the Company or to any other Investor for any claim arising out of, or based upon, (i) the investment by any Investor in any entity competitive to the Company, or (ii) actions taken by any partner, officer, or other representative of any Investor to assist any such competitive company, whether or not such action was taken as a board member of such competitive company, or otherwise, and whether or not such action has a detrimental effect on the Company.

Assignment:	Each of the Investors shall be entitled to transfer all or part of its shares of Series A Preferred purchased by it to one or more affiliated partnerships or funds managed by it or any or their respective directors, officers, or partners, provided such transferee agrees in writing to be subject to the terms of the Stock Purchase Agreement and related agreements as if it were a purchaser thereunder.
Legal Fees and Expenses:	The Company shall bear its own fees and expenses and shall pay at the closing (or in the event the transaction is not consummated, upon notice by Acme that it is terminating negotiations with respect to the consummated transactions) the reasonable fees (not to exceed $__,000) and expenses of **[our counsel]** regardless if any transactions contemplated by this term sheet are actually consummated.
Governing Law:	This summary of terms shall be governed in all respects by the laws of the State of Delaware.
Conditions Precedent to Financing:	Except for the provisions contained herein entitled "Legal Fees and Expenses," "No-Shop Agreement," "Right to Conduct Activities," and "Governing Law," which are explicitly agreed by the Investors and the Company to be binding upon execution of this term sheet, this summary of terms is not intended as a legally binding commitment by the Investors, and any obligation on the part of the Investors is subject to the following conditions precedent: 1. Completion of legal documentation satisfactory to the prospective Investors. 2. Satisfactory completion of due diligence by the prospective Investors.

3. Delivery of a customary management rights letter to Acme.

[4. Submission of detailed budget for the following twelve (12) months, acceptable to Investors.]

[5. The Company shall initiate a rights offering allowing all current "accredited" shareholders the right to participate proratably in the transactions contemplated herein.]

Finders: The Company and the Investors shall each indemnify the other for any broker's or finder's fees for which either is responsible.

Acme Counsel: **TBD**

<u>Acknowledged and agreed:</u>

ACME VENTURE CAPITAL 2011, L.P.

By: _____
Print Name: _____
Title: _____

NEWCO.COM
By: _____
Print Name: _____
Title: _____

Appendix B: Sample Letter of Intent

_____, 20__

Seller A
[Address]

_____

Re: Proposal to Purchase Stock of the Company

Dear Sellers:

This letter is intended to summarize the principal terms of a proposal being considered by _____ (the "Buyer") regarding its possible acquisition of all of the outstanding capital stock of _____ (the "Company") from _____ ("A") and _____, who are the Company's sole stockholders (the "Sellers"). In this letter, (i) the Buyer and the Sellers are sometimes called the "Parties," (ii) the Company and its subsidiaries are sometimes called the "Target Companies," and (iii) the Buyer's possible acquisition of the stock of the Company is sometimes called the "Possible Acquisition."

PART ONE

The Parties wish to commence negotiating a definitive written acquisition agreement providing for the Possible Acquisition (a "Definitive Agreement"). To facilitate the negotiation of a Definitive Agreement, the Parties request that the Buyer's counsel prepare an initial draft. The execution of any such Definitive Agreement would be subject to the satisfactory completion of the Buyer's ongoing investigation of the Target Companies' business, and would also be subject to approval by the Buyer's board of directors.

Based on the information currently known to the Buyer, it is proposed that the Definitive Agreement include the following terms:

1. **Basic Transaction**

   The Sellers would sell all of the outstanding capital stock of the Company to the Buyer at the price (the "Purchase Price") set forth in Paragraph 2 below. The closing of this transaction (the "Closing") would occur as soon as possible after the termination of the applicable waiting period under the Hart-Scott-Rodino Antitrust Improvements Act of 1976 (the "HSR Act").

2. **Purchase Price**

   The Purchase Price would be $_____ (subject to adjustment as described below) and would be paid in the following manner:

   (a) At the Closing, the Buyer would pay the Sellers the sum of $_____ in cash;

   (b) at the Closing, the Buyer would deposit with a mutually acceptable escrow agent the sum of $_____, which would be held in escrow for a period of at least _____ years in order to secure the performance of the Sellers' obligations under the Definitive Agreement and related documents; and

   (c) at the Closing, the Buyer would execute and deliver to each Seller an unsecured, nonnegotiable, subordinated promissory note. The promissory notes to be delivered to the Sellers by the Buyer would have a combined principal amount of $_____, would bear interest at the rate of __% per annum, would mature on the _____ anniversary of the Closing, and would provide for _____ equal [annual] [quarterly] payments of principal along with [annual] [quarterly] payments of accrued interest.

   The Purchase Price assumes that the Target Companies have consolidated stockholders' equity of at least $_____ as of the Closing. The Purchase Price would be adjusted based on changes in the Target Companies' consolidated stockholders' equity as of the Closing, on a dollar-for-dollar basis.

3. **Employment and Noncompetition Agreements**

   At the Closing:

   (a) the Company and A would enter into a _____-year employment agreement under which A would agree to continue to serve as the Company's [Vice President and Chief Operating Officer] and would be entitled to receive a salary of $_____ per year; and

   (b) each Seller would execute a _____-year noncompetition agreement in favor of the Buyer and the Company.

4. **Other Terms**

The Sellers would make comprehensive representations and warranties to the Buyer, and would provide comprehensive covenants, indemnities, and other protections for the benefit of the Buyer. The consummation of the contemplated transactions by the Buyer would be subject to the satisfaction of various conditions, including:

(a) _____

_____

(b) _____

_____

PART TWO

The following paragraphs of this letter (the "Binding Provisions") are the legally binding and enforceable agreements of the Buyer and each Seller.

1. **Access**

During the period from the date this letter is signed by the Sellers (the "Signing Date") until the date on which either Party provides the other Party with written notice that negotiations toward a Definitive Agreement are terminated (the "Termination Date"), the Sellers will afford the Buyer full and free access to each Target Company, its personnel, properties, contracts, books, and records, and all other documents and data.

2. **Exclusive Dealing**

Until the later of (i) [90] days after the Signing Date or (ii) the Termination Date:

(a) the Sellers will not and will cause the Target Companies not to, directly or indirectly, through any representative or otherwise, solicit or entertain offers from, negotiate with or in any manner encourage, discuss, accept, or consider any proposal of any other person relating to the acquisition of the Shares or the Target Companies, their assets or business, in whole or in part, whether directly or indirectly, through purchase, merger, consolidation, or otherwise (other than sales of inventory in the ordinary course); and

(b) the Sellers will immediately notify the Buyer regarding any contact between the Sellers, any Target Company or their respective representatives, and any other person regarding any such offer or proposal or any related inquiry.

3. **Breakup Fee**

If (a) the Sellers breach Paragraph 2 or the Sellers provide to the Buyer written notice that negotiations toward a Definitive Agreement are terminated, and (b) within [six] months after the date of such breach or the Termination Date, as the case may be, either Seller or one or more of the Target Companies signs a letter of intent or other agreement relating to the acquisition of a material portion of the Shares or of the Target Companies, their assets, or business, in whole or in part, whether directly or indirectly, through purchase, merger, consolidation, or otherwise (other than sales of inventory or immaterial portions of the Target Companies' assets in the ordinary course) and such transaction is ultimately consummated, then, immediately upon the closing of such transaction, the Sellers will pay, or cause the Target Companies to pay, to the Buyer the sum $_____. This fee will not serve as the exclusive remedy to the Buyer under this letter in the event of a breach by the Sellers of Paragraph 2 of this Part Two or any other of the Binding Provisions, and the Buyer will be entitled to all other rights and remedies provided by law or in equity.

4. **Conduct of Business**

During the period from the Signing Date until the Termination Date, the Sellers shall cause the Target Companies to operate their business in the ordinary course and to refrain from any extraordinary transactions.

5. **Confidentiality**

Except as and to the extent required by law, the Buyer will not disclose or use, and will direct its representatives not to disclose or use to the detriment of the Sellers or the Target Companies, any Confidential Information (as defined below) with respect to the Target Companies furnished, or to be furnished, by either Seller, the Target Companies, or their respective representatives to the Buyer or its representatives at any time or in any manner other than in connection with its evaluation of the transaction proposed in this letter. For purposes of this Paragraph, "Confidential Information" means any information about the Target Companies stamped "confidential" or identified in writing as such to the Buyer by the Sellers promptly following its disclosure, unless (i) such information is already known to the Buyer or its representatives or to others not bound by a duty of confidentiality or such information becomes publicly available through no fault of the Buyer or its representatives, (ii) the use of such information is necessary or appropriate in making any filing or obtaining any consent or approval required for the consummation of the Possible Acquisition, or (iii) the furnishing or use of such information is required by or necessary or appropriate in connection with legal proceedings. Upon the written request of the Sellers, the Buyer will promptly return to the Sellers or the Target Companies or destroy any Confidential Information in its possession and certify in writing to the Sellers that it has done so.

6. **Disclosure**

Except as and to the extent required by law, without the prior written consent of the other Party, neither the Buyer nor the Seller will make, and each will direct its representatives not to make, directly or indirectly, any public comment, statement, or communication with respect to, or otherwise to disclose or to permit the disclosure of the existence of discussions regarding, a possible transaction between the Parties or any of the terms, conditions, or other aspects of the transaction proposed in this letter. If a Party is required by law to make any such disclosure, it must first provide to the other Party the content of the proposed disclosure, the reasons that such disclosure is required by law, and the time and place that the disclosure will be made.

7. **Costs**

The Buyer and each Seller will be responsible for and bear all of its own costs and expenses (including any broker's or finder's fees and the expenses of its representatives) incurred at any time in connection with pursuing or consummating the Possible Acquisition. Notwithstanding the preceding sentence, the Buyer will pay one-half and the Sellers will pay one-half of the HSR Act filing fee.

8. **Consents**

During the period from the Signing Date until the Termination Date, the Buyer and each Seller will cooperate with each other and proceed, as promptly as is reasonably practical, to prepare and to file the notifications required by the HSR Act.

9. **Entire Agreement**

The Binding Provisions constitute the entire agreement between the parties, and supersede all prior oral or written agreements, understandings, representations and warranties, and courses of conduct and dealing between the parties on the subject matter hereof. Except as otherwise provided herein, the Binding Provisions may be amended or modified only by a writing executed by all of the parties.

10. **Governing Law**

The Binding Provisions will be governed by and construed under the laws of the State of _____ without regard to conflicts of laws principles.

11. **Jurisdiction: Service of Process**

Any action or proceeding seeking to enforce any provision of, or based on any right arising out of, this Letter may be brought against any of the parties in the courts of the State of _____, County of _____, or, if it has or can acquire jurisdiction, in the United States District Court for the _____ District of _____, and each of the parties consents to the jurisdiction of such courts (and of the appropriate appellate courts) in any such action or proceeding and waives any objection to venue laid therein. Process in any action or proceeding referred to in the preceding sentence may be served on any party anywhere in the world.

12. **Termination**

The Binding Provisions will automatically terminate on _____, 20___ and may be terminated earlier upon written notice by either party to the other party unilaterally, for any reason or no reason, with or without cause, at any time; provided, however, that the termination of the Binding Provisions will not affect the liability of a party for breach of any of the Binding Provisions prior to the termination. Upon termination of the Binding Provisions, the parties will have no further obligations hereunder, except as stated in Paragraphs 2, 3, 5, 7, 9, 10, 11, 12, 13, and 14 of this Part Two, which will survive any such termination.

13. Counterparts

This Letter may be executed in one or more counterparts, each of which will be deemed to be an original copy of this Letter and all of which, when taken together, will be deemed to constitute one and the same agreement.

14. No Liability

The paragraphs and provisions of Part One of this letter do not constitute and will not give rise to any legally binding obligation on the part of any of the Parties or any of the Target Companies. Moreover, except as expressly provided in the Binding Provisions (or as expressly provided in any binding written agreement that the Parties may enter into in the future), no past or future action, course of conduct, or failure to act relating to the Possible Acquisition, or relating to the negotiation of the terms of the Possible Acquisition or any Definitive Agreement, will give rise to or serve as a basis for any obligation or other liability on the part of the Parties or any of the Target Companies.

If you are in agreement with the foregoing, please sign and return one copy of this letter agreement, which thereupon will constitute our agreement with respect to its subject matter.

Very truly yours,

BUYER:

By: _____

Name: _____

Title: _____

Duly executed and agreed as to the Binding Provisions on _____, 20__.

PROSPECTIVE SELLERS:

_____

_____

Appendix C: Additional Resources

Over the past few years there has been a Cambrian explosion of entrepreneurial resources, including many around financing a company. Following are several important ones.

Accelerators Accelerators modeled after TechStars (www .techstars.com) and Y Combinator (http://ycombinator .com) have emerged all over the world. These programs typically invest a modest amount of money (around $20,000) in companies in exchange for a small amount of equity (typically 6 percent). The companies then go through a 90-day, intensive, full-time program where they accelerate their start-up via help from the accelerator, mentors, and the surrounding start-up community. Several years ago, TechStars founded the Global Accelerator Network (http://globalacceleratornet work.com) in an effort to link the best accelerators and provide a series of best practices across them. Recently, several corporate accelerators, such as the Microsoft Accelerator (www.microsoft.com/bizspark/accelerator) have begun appearing.

Angel and Seed Listing Web Sites If you are an entrepreneur raising money or are an angel or seed VC looking for seed or early stage investments, there are a number of websites that are effectively a listing or matching service for you. The two most popular ones, AngelList (www.angel.co) and Gust (www.gust.com), have become very powerful resources for both entrepreneurs and investors.

Ask the VC (www.askthevc.com) This is the companion web site for *Venture Deals* and is maintained by us. On it we have a regularly updated blog where we answer questions submitted via the web site as well as highlight great blog posts by other VCs. We include the Foundry Group form documents, other forms of financing documents, and sample mergers and acquisitions (M&A) documents on the site. We also have a list of many college courses that use *Venture Deals* along with the syllabus for these courses. We anticipate releasing a university-level teaching manual for this book and including additional resources on this site for educators in late 2012.

Crowd Funding Crowd funding is a new form of financing that has been enabled by the Internet. Popular sites like KickStarter (www.kickstarter.com) and Indiegogo (www.indiegogo.com) have popularized the first phase of this, where companies can use crowd funding to raise money to build their products. In the current model, companies are effectively getting their customers to prepay for their product or service. In April 2012 in the United States, the Jumpstart Our Business Startups (JOBS) Act was passed, which provides for equity crowd funding, or the ability of a company to use the notion of crowd funding to raise equity. The specific laws around this are still being worked on at the time of this writing, but we expect crowd funding to be an impactful form of financing for early stage companies. Regardless of the final rules, we always suggest that you know who is investing in your company and what motivates them to invest.

Crunchbase If you are looking for information about which companies are being funded by whom, Crunchbase (www.crunchbase.com) is the best free resource that we know of. Keep in mind that with all private company data, accuracy varies a lot, so you'll find some noise here; but in general the signal is high. If you don't have a strong VC network, Crunchbase can help you identify the VCs who might be interested in your particular company.

Education There is an enormous amount of entrepreneurship-oriented educational resources on the Web. Several of our favorites include the Kauffman Foundation (www.kauffman.org), Stanford University's Entrepreneurship Corner (http://ecorner.stanford.edu), Khan Academy's venture capital courses (www.khanacademy.org/finance-economics/venture-capital-and-capital-markets?k), and the Silicon Flatirons Center right here in our hamlet of Boulder, Colorado (www.siliconflatirons.com).

National Venture Capital Association The NVCA (www.nvca.org) maintains the most widely used set of model documents used in financings. If you are confused about a term that we do not discuss in this book, take a look at the NVCA site (http://nvca.org/index.php?option=com_content&view=article&id =108&Itemid=136), as it addresses every term that we've ever seen in a term sheet, even the egregious ones.

Other Tech Blogs There are numerous tech and VC bloggers who produce significant amounts of excellent content. We list all VC bloggers we are aware of on the right side of Ask the VC (www.askthevc.com). Several of our good friends, including Fred Wilson (www.avc.com), Mark Suster (www .bothsidesofthetable.com), David Cohen (www.davidgcohen .com/blog), and Seth Levine (www.sethlevine.com), regularly produce excellent content. Brownstein & Egusa (www .brownsteinegusa.com/find-tech-reporters) also has an extensive list of tech reporters and bloggers.

Startup America The Startup America Partnership (www.s.co) was created in 2010 based on the simple premise that young companies that grow create jobs. Today, thousands of companies are taking advantage of the resources provided by Startup America, and at the time of this writing over 30 states have created Startup Regions (for example, Startup Colorado at www.startupcolorado.com).

Glossary

accelerator A program intended to mentor and accelerate the growth and success of a startup company.

accredited investor As defined by federal securities laws, this is a person who is permitted to invest in startups and other high-risk private company securities.

acquisition A transaction between two companies where one is buying the other.

adverse change redemption A type of redemption right whereby a shareholder gets the right to redeem his shares if something adverse happens to the company.

advisers People who advise startup companies. Normally these people are paid some sort of compensation for their efforts.

analyst A very junior person at a VC firm, often a recent college graduate.

angel investor An individual who provides capital to a startup company. This person is usually independently wealthy and invests his own money in the company.

antidilution A term that provides price protection for investors. This is accomplished by effectively repricing an investor's shares to a lower price per share in the event that the company completes a financing at a lower valuation than a previous financing round.

as-converted basis Looking at the equity base of the company assuming that all preferred stock has been converted to common.

associate A person at a VC firm who is involved in deal analysis and management. The seniority of this position varies by firm, but generally associates need a partner to support their activities.

at-will employee An employee who does not have an employment agreement and can be terminated by the company for any reason.

barter element The price at which a stock option may be exercised.

basis of stock option The price at which a stock option may be exercised.

best alternative to negotiated agreement (BATNA) A backup plan if no agreement is reached between two parties.

blended preferences When all classes of preferred stock have equivalent payment rights in a liquidation.

bridge loan A loan given to a company by investors with the intent that the money will fund the company to the next equity financing.

broad-based antidilution The denominator in weighted average antidilution calculations that takes into consideration a fully diluted view of the company. The opposite is called a narrow-based antidilution.

cap The valuation ceiling that exists in a convertible debt deal.

capital call The method by which a VC fund asks its investors to contribute their pro rata portion of money being called by a VC fund to make investments, pay expenses, or pay management fees.

capitalization table (cap table) A spreadsheet that defines the economics of a deal. It contains a detailed description of all the owners of stock of a company.

carry/carried interest The profits that VCs are entitled to after returning capital committed to their investors. This typically ranges from 20 percent to 30 percent.

carve-out (equity) The concept whereby shareholders agree to give a preferential payment (usually to executives and employees of a company) ahead of the shareholders agreeing to the carve-out. Normally, one would see a carve-out used in the situation where liquidation preferences are such that employees of the company do not have enough financial interests in a liquidation event.

carve-out (merger) Within the merger context, these are certain representations and warranties that will be indemnified outside of the escrow.

clawback The provision in the limited partnership agreement that allows investors to take back money from the VC should they overpay themselves with carry.

commitment period The length of time a VC fund has to find and invest in new companies, usually five years.

common stock The type of stock that has the least amount of rights, privileges, and preferences. Normally employees and founders of a company hold common stock, as the price they pay for the stock can be much less than that of preferred stock.

control Terms that allow a VC to exert positive or veto control in a deal.

conversion price adjustment The mechanism by which an antidilution adjustment takes place. This allows the preferred stock to be converted into more common stock than originally agreed upon and thus allows the preferred to own more stock and voting rights upon converting to common.

convertible debt A debt or loan instrument that an investor gives to a company with the intent that it will convert later to equity and not be paid back as a standard bank loan would be.

cross-fund investment When a VC firm operates more than one fund and more than one fund invests in the same company.

director A junior deal partner at a VC firm.

double-trigger acceleration A term that describes the situation in which a person would receive accelerated vesting. In a double-trigger situation, two events would trigger accelerated vesting, such as a merger of the company followed by a termination of a person's employment.

down round A financing round that is at a lower valuation than the previous round.

drag-along agreement A term that sets up a proxy on one's stock ownership to vote the same way as others do on a particular issue.

due diligence The process by which investors explore a company that they are thinking of investing in.

earn-out An amount agreed upon by an acquirer and a target company that the former shareholders of the target company will get if certain performance milestones are met post merger.

economics Terms that impact the returns of a VC's investment in a company.

employee pool The shares set aside by a company to provide stock options to employees.

entrepreneur Someone who creates a new company, also known as a startup.

entrepreneur in residence (EIR) A person at a venture firm that is usually a former entrepreneur who is helping out the venture firm finding deals to invest in, or working on his next company that the venture firm will one day fund.

equity Ownership in a company.

escrow The amount of consideration that an acquiring company holds back following a merger to make sure that representations and warranties made by the purchased company are true.

escrow cap The amount of money in a merger that is set aside to remedy breaches of the merger agreement.

executive managing director A senior partner in a VC firm who is superior to a managing director or general partner.

executive summary A short summary document, normally one to three pages, that describes material facts and strategies of a company.

exercise The act of purchasing stock pursuant to a stock option or warrant.

fair market value The price that a third party would pay for something in the open market.

fiduciary duties A legal and ethical duty that an individual has to an entity.

flat round A financing round done at the same postmoney valuation as that of the previous round.

founder Someone who creates a new company, also known as a startup.

founding general partner A senior partner in a VC firm who founded the firm.

fully diluted A term explicitly defining that all rights to purchase equity should be in the valuation calculation.

game theory The concept that one's actions depend on what actions other persons may or may not take and the inherent incentives behind these actions.

general partner (GP) A senior partner in a VC firm.

general partnership (GP) The entity that manages the limited partnership.

GP commitment The amount of money, usually between 1 percent and 5 percent of the fund, that the general partners invest in their own fund.

holdback The amount of consideration that an acquiring company holds back following a merger to make sure that representations and warranties made by the purchased company are true.

indemnification The promise by one party to protect another party should something go wrong.

investment term The length of time that a VC fund can remain active, typically 10 years with two one-year extensions.

key man clause Contractual provision within the limited partnership agreement that describes what will happen if certain partners leave the VC fund.

lead investor The investor in a startup company who takes on the leadership position in a VC financing.

letter of intent (LOI) A term sheet for a merger.

light preferred A version of a preferred stock financing that has very simple and watered-down terms.

limited partners (LPs) The investors in a VC fund.

limited partnership (LP) The entity used by the limited partners to invest in a VC fund.

limited partnership agreement (LPA) The contract between a VC fund and its investors.

liquidation event/liquidity event When a company is sold and ceases to exist as a stand-alone company.

liquidation preference A right given to a class of preferred stock allowing that stock to receive proceeds in a liquidation in advance of other classes of stock.

major investor A concept used in VC financings that allows a company to distinguish between shareholders who purchase more stock than others.

management company The entity that services each fund that a VC raises.

management fee The fee that the VC funds have a right to receive from their LPs as money to manage their business operations regardless of the performance of the fund.

managing director (MD) A senior partner in a VC firm.

materiality qualifiers Inserting the word *material* in front of things such as protective provisions.

mentors People who advise startup companies or their executives. Normally these people are not paid.

micro VC A super angel who raises a small fund made up of professional investors.

multiplay game A term in game theory that deals with a game or situation where there is a continuing relationship after the game is played, like a VC financing whereby after the transaction is completed the VC and the entrepreneur will join forces to work together.

nondisclosure agreement (NDA) An agreement whereby one party promises not to share information of another party.

operating partner A position at a VC firm that is normally under managing director, but above principal.

option budget The amount of options a company plans to allocate to employees over a finite time period.

option pool The shares set aside by a company to provide stock options to employees.

pari passu When all classes of preferred stock have equivalent payment rights in a liquidation.

pay-to-play A term that forces VCs to continue to invest in future company financings or suffer adverse consequences to their ownership positions.

postmoney The value of a company after an investor has put money into the company.

preferred stock A type of stock that has preferential terms, rights, and privileges compared to common stock.

premoney The value ascribed to a company by an investor before investing in the company.

price per share The dollar amount assigned to purchase one share of stock.

principal A junior deal partner at a VC firm.

private placement memorandum (PPM) A long legal document that is prepared by the company, its bankers, and its lawyers that is a long-form business plan created to solicit investors.

pro rata right The right of a shareholder to purchase shares in a future financing equal to the percentage the shareholder currently holds at the time of such financing.

protective provisions Contractual rights that allow the holders of preferred stock to vote on certain important matters pertaining to a company.

ratchet-based antidilution A style of antidilution that reprices an investor's shares in previous rounds, usually through a conversion price adjustment, to the price paid in the current round.

representations and warranties Provisions in a financing purchase agreement or merger agreement whereby the company makes certain assurances about itself.

reserves The amount of money that a VC firm allocates on its books for future investments to a particular portfolio company.

reverse dilution The situation in which stock is returned to a company by departed employees whose stock has not vested, thus increasing the effective ownership of all shareholders in a company.

right of rescission The right of shareholders to force the company to buy back their stock, usually given to people who were not supposed to buy the stock in the first place under federal securities law.

safe harbor A legally defined way of escaping liability under a law if a party performs certain acts as defined by such law.

secondary sale The sale by a VC of stock in a portfolio company or its entire portfolio to an outside party in a private transaction.

seed preferred Same as light preferred: A simple watered-down version of a preferred stock financing.

seed stage A startup that is in its infancy.

Series A financing The first or early round of financing that a company raises.

Series Seed financing A small financing that occurs before the Series A financing and is often the very first financing of a company.

single-play game A term in game theory that deals with a game or situation in which there is no continuing relationship after the game is played.

single-trigger acceleration A term used to describe the situation (e.g., a merger) in which a person would receive accelerated vesting.

stacked preference When different classes of preferred stock have senior rights to payment over other classes of preferred stock.

stock option A right to purchase shares of stock in a company.

strike price The price at which a stock option may be exercised.

super angel A very active and experienced angel investor.

super pro rata rights The right of shareholders to purchase shares in a future financing equal to some multiple of the percentage they currently hold at the time of such financing.

syndicate The group of investors who invest in a startup.

term sheet A summary document of key terms in contemplation of a financing.

valuation The value ascribed to a company by an investor.

VC fund The entities that make up the investment family of a VC.

venture capitalist (VC) A person who invests in startup companies.

venture partner A position at a VC firm that is normally under managing director, but above principal.

warrant A right to purchase shares of stock in a company.

weighted average antidilution A style of antidilution that reprices an investor's investment, usually through a conversion price adjustment, to a lower price per share, but takes into account the relative effect of the amount of shares sold in the current round.

zone of insolvency When a company is nearly insolvent and doesn't have the assets to pay off its liabilities.

About the Authors

Brad Feld (brad@foundrygroup.com, @bfeld, www.feld.com) is a co-founder and managing director of Foundry Group, a Boulder, Colorado–based early stage venture capital fund. Foundry Group invests in information technology companies all over the United States.

Prior to co-founding Foundry Group, Brad co-founded Mobius Venture Capital and, prior to that, founded Intensity Ventures, a company that helped launch and operate software companies. Brad is also a co-founder of TechStars and co-authored the book *Do More Faster: TechStars Lessons to Accelerate Your Startup.*

Previously, Brad served as chief technology officer of Ameri-Data Technologies. AmeriData acquired Feld Technologies, a firm he founded in 1987 that specialized in custom software applications. Brad had grown Feld Technologies into one of Boston's leading software consulting firms prior to the acquisition. He also directed the diversification into software consulting at AmeriData, a $1.5 billion publicly traded company that was acquired by GE Capital in 1995.

In addition to his investing efforts, Brad has been active with several nonprofit organizations and currently is chairman of the National Center for Women and Information Technology. Brad is a nationally recognized speaker on the topics of venture capital investing and entrepreneurship and writes widely read and well-respected blogs at www.feld.com and www.askthevc.com.

Brad holds bachelor of science and master of science degrees in management science from the Massachusetts Institute of Technology. He is also an avid art collector and long-distance runner. He has completed 22 marathons as part of his mission to run a marathon in each of the 50 states.

Jason Mendelson (jason@foundrygroup.com, @jasonmendelson, www.jasonmendelson.com) is a co-founder and managing director of Foundry Group, a Boulder, Colorado–based early stage venture capital fund. Foundry Group invests in information technology companies all over the United States.

Prior to co-founding Foundry Group, Jason was a managing director and general counsel for Mobius Venture Capital, where he also acted as its chief administrative partner overseeing all operations of the firm.

Prior to his involvement with Mobius Venture Capital, Jason was an attorney with Cooley LLP, where he practiced corporate and securities law with an emphasis on representation of emerging companies in private and public financings, mergers, and acquisitions. As an attorney, Jason has consummated over $2 billion of venture capital investments and $5 billion in mergers and has had extensive experience in fund formation, employment law, and general litigation, serving as an expert witness in these related fields.

Before his legal career, Jason was a senior consultant and software engineer at Accenture.

As one of the first full-time, in-house general counsels at a venture capital firm, Jason has been at the forefront of thought leadership; he has co-chaired the National Venture Capital Association's General Counsel group and has been an active participant on the NVCA's Chief Financial Officer group. He was one of the key draftspersons for the NVCA model document task force, which created the industry's first set of standardized venture capital financing documents, which has greatly aided in the efficiency of completing these types of deals. He currently sits on the board of the NVCA.

Jason holds a bachelor of arts degree in economics, and a juris doctorate from the University of Michigan. He is an active musician, playing drums and bass guitar in several bands; he also enjoys home remodeling, food, and travel. Jason blogs about his experiences in the venture industry on his blogs at www.jasonmendelson.com and on www.askthevc.com.

Index

CHAPTER THREE

PRINCIPLES OF A VIBRANT STARTUP COMMUNITY

Now that you've had an introduction to Boulder and its history from my point of view, I'd like to describe the principles that drive the Boulder startup community, which I'll call the Boulder Thesis. First, however, I'll discuss the three historical frameworks that have been used to describe why some cities become vibrant startup communities.

HISTORICAL FRAMEWORKS

The investigation into startup communities is among the most important inquiries of our time. Why do some places flourish with innovation while others wither? What are the determinants that help a startup community achieve critical startup mass? Once under way, how does a startup community sustain and expand entrepreneurship? Why do startup communities persist, despite often having higher real estate costs and wages than other areas? At stake is nothing less than the continued economic vitality, and even the very existence of towns, cities, and regions.

Studies show that the geography of innovation is neither democratic nor flat. This may be surprising since you might think that location should matter less than ever in today's society. Information can be quickly sent and received by anyone from almost anywhere. In theory, expanding access to resources and information from anywhere might decouple the relationship between place and innovation.

Economic geographers, however, observe the opposite effect. Evidence suggests that location, rather than being irrelevant, is more important than ever. Innovation tilts heavily toward certain locations and, as scholar Richard Florida (professor at Rotman School of Management, at the University of Toronto and author of *The Rise of the Creative Class* (2002)) says, is "spiky" with great concentration of creative, innovative people in tightly clustered geographies. Location clearly matters.

Three prominent frameworks explain why some locales are hotbeds of entrepreneurship whereas others are the innovation equivalent of a twenty-first century economic mirage. Each explanation of regional entrepreneurial advantage comes from a different discipline—one from economics, another from sociology, and a third from geography. These explanations are, for the most part, nonexclusive and complementary.

The first explanation, *external or agglomeration economies*, comes from economics. This line of analysis reaches back to the research of economist Alfred Marshall, and, in recent decades, Michael Porter, Paul Krugman, and Paul Romer have deepened this account. External economies focus on the benefits of startup concentration in an area. This explanation focuses on economic concepts as they apply to location. One is that companies co-located in an area benefit from "external economies of scale." Emerging companies need certain common inputs—for example, infrastructure, specialized legal and accounting services, suppliers, labor pools with a specialized knowledge base—that reside outside the company. Companies in a common geographic area share the fixed costs of these resources external to the company. As more and more startups in an area can share the costs of specialized inputs, the average cost per startup drops for the specialized inputs. This provides direct economic benefit to companies located within a startup community.

Another economic concept, *network effects*, explains why geographic concentration yields further advantage. Network effects operate in systems where the addition of a member to a network enhances value for existing users. The Internet, Facebook, and Twitter are examples in which network effects operate powerfully. These services may have some value to you if there are just 100 other users. However, these networks are immensely more useful if there are 100 million other users that you can connect with. Startup communities similarly feature strong network effects. For example, an area with 10 great programmers provides a valuable pool of labor talent for a startup. However, an additional 1,000 amazing programmers in the same area is vastly more valuable to startups, especially if programmers share best practices with other programmers, inspire one another, or start new companies. External economies of scale lower certain costs; meanwhile, network effects make co-location more valuable.

The second explanation of startup communities, *horizontal networks*, comes from sociology. In her PhD work at MIT, AnnaLee Saxenian (currently Dean of the UC Berkeley School of Information) noticed that external economies do not fully explain the development and adaptation of startup communities. In particular, in her seminal book *Regional Advantage: Culture and Competition in Silicon Valley and Route 128* (1994) Saxenian noted that two hotbeds for high-tech activity—Silicon Valley and Boston's Route 128—looked very similar in the mid-1980s. Each area enjoyed agglomeration economies associated with the nation's two high-tech regions. Yet just a decade later, Silicon Valley gained a dominant advantage over Route 128. External economies alone did not provide an answer. Saxenian set out to resolve the puzzle of why Silicon Valley far outpaced Route 128 from the mid-1980s to mid-1990s.

Saxenian persuasively argues that a culture of openness and information exchange fueled Silicon Valley's ascent over Route 128. This argument is tied to network effects, which are better leveraged by a community with a culture of information sharing across companies and industries. Saxenian observed that the porous boundaries between Silicon Valley companies, such as Sun Microsystems and HP, stood in stark contrast to the closed-loop and autarkic companies of Route 128, such as DEC and Apollo. More broadly, Silicon Valley culture embraced a horizontal exchange of information across and between companies. Rapid technological disruption played perfectly to Silicon Valley's culture of open information exchange and labor mobility. As technology quickly changed, the Silicon Valley companies were better positioned to share information, adopt new trends, leverage innovation, and nimbly respond to new conditions. Meanwhile, vertical integration and closed systems disadvantaged many Route 128 companies during periods of technological upheaval. Saxenian highlights the role of a densely networked culture in explaining Silicon Valley's successful industrial adaptation as compared to Route 128.

Finally, the third explanation of startup communities, the notion of the *creative class*, comes from geography. Richard Florida describes the tie between innovation and creative-class individuals. The creative class is composed of individuals such as entrepreneurs, engineers, professors, and artists who create "meaningful new forms." Creative-class individuals, Florida argues, want to live in nice places, enjoy a culture with a tolerance for new ideas and weirdness, and—most of all—want to be around other creative-class individuals. This is another example of network effects, because a virtuous cycle exists where the existence of a creative class in an area attracts more creative-class individuals to the area, which in turn makes the area even more valuable and attractive. A location that hits critical mass enjoys a competitive geographic advantage over places that have yet to attract a significant number of creative-class individuals.

Each of the three explanations just outlined provides a useful lens to understand why the entrepreneurial world has concentrations of startup communities in specific geographies. They are incomplete, however, concerning how to put a startup community into motion. There is a serious chicken and egg problem; although it is not difficult to see why innovation havens have an advantage, it is more challenging to explain how to get a startup community up and running.

THE BOULDER THESIS

I suggest a fourth framework based on our experience in Boulder. Let's call it the Boulder Thesis. This framework has four key components:

1. Entrepreneurs must lead the startup community.
2. The leaders must have a long-term commitment.
3. The startup community must be inclusive of anyone who wants to participate in it.
4. The startup community must have continual activities that engage the entire entrepreneurial stack.

LED BY ENTREPRENEURS

The most critical principle of a startup community is that entrepreneurs must lead it. Lots of different people are involved in the startup community and many nonentrepreneurs play key roles. Unless the entrepreneurs lead, the startup community will not be sustainable over time.

In virtually every major city, there are long lists of different types of people and organizations who are involved in the startup community including government, universities, investors, mentors, and service providers. Historically, many of these organizations try to play a leadership role in the development of their local startup community. Although their involvement is important, they can't be the leaders. The entrepreneurs have to be leaders.

I define an entrepreneur as someone who has co-founded a company. I differentiate between "high-growth entrepreneurial companies" and "small businesses." Both are important, but they are different things. Entrepreneurial companies have the potential to be or are high-growth businesses whereas small businesses tend to be local, profitable, but slow-growth organizations. Small-business people are often "pillars of their community" as their businesses have a tight co-dependency with their community. By contrast, founders of high-growth entrepreneurial companies generally are involved in the local community as employers and indirect contributors to small businesses and the local economy, but they rarely are involved in the broad business community because they are extraordinarily focused on their companies.

Because of this intense focus, it's unrealistic to think that all entrepreneurs in a community will be leaders. All that is needed is a critical mass of entrepreneurs, often less than a dozen, who will provide leadership.

LONG-TERM COMMITMENT

These leaders have to make a long-term commitment to their startup community. I like to say this has to be at least 20 years from today to reinforce the sense that this has to be meaningful in length. Optimally, the commitment resets daily; it should be a forward-looking 20-year commitment.

It's well understood that economies run in cycles. Economies grow, peak, decline, bottom out, grow again, peak again, decline again, and bottom out again. Some of these cycles are modest. Some are severe. The lengths vary dramatically.

Startup communities have to take a very long-term view. A great startup community such as Silicon Valley (1950–today) has a long trajectory. Although they have their booms and busts, they continued to grow, develop, and expand throughout this period of time.

Most cities and their leaders get excited about entrepreneurship after a major economic decline. They focus on it for a few years through a peak.

When the subsequent decline ultimately happens, they focus on other things during the downturn. When things bottom out, most of the progress gained during the upswing was lost. I've seen this several times—first in the early 1990s and again around the Internet bubble. All you have to do is think back to the nickname of your city during the Internet bubble (Silicon Alley, Silicon Swamp, Silicon Slopes, Silicon Prairie, Silicon Gulch, and Silicon Mountain) to remember what it was like before and after the peak.

This is why the leaders have to first be entrepreneurs and then have a long-term view. These leaders must be committed to the continuous development of their startup community, regardless of the economic cycle their city, state, or country is in. Great entrepreneurial companies, such as Apple, Genentech, Microsoft, and Intel, were started during down economic cycles. It takes such a long time to create something powerful that, almost by definition, you'll go through several economic cycles on the path to glory.

If you aspire to be a leader of your startup community, but you aren't willing to live where you are for the next 20 years and work hard at leading the startup community for that period of time, ask yourself what your real motivation for being a leader is. Although you can have impact for a shorter period of time, it'll take at least this level of commitment from some leaders to sustain a vibrant startup community.

FOSTER A PHILOSOPHY OF INCLUSIVENESS

A startup community must be extremely inclusive. Anyone who wants to engage should be able to, whether they are changing careers, moving to your city, graduating from college, or just want to do something different. This applies to entrepreneurs, people who want to work for startups, people who want to work with startups, or people who are simply intellectually interested in startups.

This philosophy of inclusiveness applies at all levels of the startup community. The leaders have to be open to having more leaders involved, recognizing that leaders need to be entrepreneurs who have a long-term view of building their startup community. Entrepreneurs in the community need to welcome other entrepreneurs, viewing the growth of the startup community as a positive force for all, rather than a zero-sum game in which new entrepreneurs compete locally for resources and status. Employees of startups need to recruit their friends and open their homes and city to other people who have moved into the community.

Everyone in the startup community should have a perspective that having more people engaged in the startup community is good for the startup community. Building a startup community is not a zero-sum game in which there are winners and losers; if everyone engages, they and the entire community can all be winners.

ENGAGE THE ENTIRE ENTREPRENEURIAL STACK

Startup communities must have regular activities that engage the entire entrepreneurial stack. This includes first-time entrepreneurs, experienced entrepreneurs, aspiring entrepreneurs, investors, mentors, employees of startups, service providers to startups, and anyone else who wants to be involved.

Over the years, I've been to many entrepreneurial award events, periodic cocktail parties, monthly networking events, panel discussions, and open houses. Although these types of activities have a role, typically in shining a bright light on the people doing good things within the startup community, they don't really engage anyone in any real entrepreneurial activity.

The emergence of hackathons, new tech meetups, open coffee clubs, startup weekends, and accelerators like TechStars stand out in stark contrast. These are activities and events, which I will cover in depth later in this book, that last from a few hours to three months and provide a tangible, focused, set of activities for the members of the startup community to engage in. By being inclusive of the startup community, these activities consistently engage the entire entrepreneurial stack.

Some of these activities will last for decades; others will go strong for a few years and then fade away; others will fail to thrive and die quickly. This dynamic is analogous to startups—it's okay to try things that fail, and the startup community must recognize when something isn't working and move on. The leaders of the failed activity should try again to create things that engage the entire entrepreneurial stack, and participants in failed activities should keep on engaging in stuff, recognizing that they are playing a long-term game.